# GODS & HEROES

## ON THE TRAIL OF THE ILIAD & THE ODYSSEY

JILL DUDLEY

*Published by*
Orpington Publishers

*Origination by*
Creeds Design & Print Ltd.,
Bridport, Dorset
01308 423411

*Cover design and maps by*
Creeds Design & Print Ltd.



ISBN 10: 0-9553834-7-1
ISBN 13: 978-0-9553834-7-2

# CONTENTS

# PROLOGUE

The idea for *Gods & Heroes* first filtered into my mind while on the Aegean island of Chios. I remember well its gradual manifestation as we travelled round the island. Chios claims Homer as its citizen, and the islanders say it was there he sang the *Iliad* and the *Odyssey* while accompanying himself on the lyre, so what better place for this seed of an idea to germinate and take root?

Harry, when I told him I had another book in mind which would require more travel, eyed me thoughtfully and remarked that in that case I'd better get on with it while I still had my health and faculties. He was remarkably good-natured about it and, after recovering from the initial blow to his hopes of an easy life, rather surprisingly became quite enthusiastic; he had always shown an interest in battles, so I was on to a good thing with the Trojan War.

My intention in writing this book was not to join in academic arguments about whether the Trojan War was a historical fact or not, or whether the characters were real or fictional, but to travel to the places mentioned in the *Iliad* and the *Odyssey*, in other words to Troy and Greece.

Every journey has been fascinating, and I hope after reading *Gods & Heroes* anyone of a non-academic mind will find himself fired up to read Homer's two masterpieces for himself – the first ever literary compositions of the western world; and for those who already know these epic stories, that this book will encourage them to visit the places I have written about to see for themselves where the battles took place, and the remains of the palaces of the great warriors.

In order to simplify things for the reader I never vary the spelling or use alternative names for regions, towns, gods or people as has been done by Homer and by his translators. For instance, I always use the word 'Greeks', never the alternatives such as Argives, Danaans, or Achaeans; and I stick to one spelling only of any name such as Patroclus, never Patroklos, and Hecuba never Hekabe, and so on. A Glossary at the end of the book will help anyone who is unfamiliar with the gods or the Greek and Trojan heroes.

Because Homer's descriptive powers are inspirational, I often quote from him but, as the many translations vary, I have selected passages from whichever version I myself have liked the best. Most of the quotations are pre-copyright, but those that I've used which are still under legal copyright I've followed up with the initials of the translator in brackets.

The block of text before each chapter which I call my 'preludes', give a more detailed background to the myths and traditionally accepted beliefs concerning the subject of that chapter. They can be ignored altogether as what is necessary is also in the chapter.

So *Gods & Heroes* is now done and, looking back, the journeys and experiences have been exciting, sometimes challenging and certainly worthwhile. I think divine intervention (despite my own religious scepticism) has given me assistance because, without some sort of unseen hand inspiring me, and a driving force spurring me on, this book could never have been started, let alone finished.

GALLIPOLI PENINSULA
HELLESPONT
SIDGEUM
TROY
TURKEY
TÉNEDOS
RIVER SCAMANDER
BEŞIK BAY
MT. IDA
AEGEAN SEA
EDREMIT
GÜLPINAR
GULF OF EDREMIT
AYVALIK
LESBOS
MYTILENE
N
W
E
S
IZMIR

# TURKEY

# THE JUDGEMENT OF PARIS

The Judgement of Paris came about as a direct result of the marriage of Achilles' parents, King Peleus of Phthia and Thetis, a semi-divine sea-nymph. Their wedding was a great affair which took place on Mt. Pelion in north-east Thessaly to which all the immortals were invited except Eris (Strife/Discord). In a fit of pique she came anyway and, intent on causing maximum trouble, she cast down amongst the guests a golden apple on which was written 'for the fairest'. In order to prevent a rumpus at the wedding, Zeus instructed his messenger-son Hermes to take the apple far away from the celebrations, and bring it to Mt. Ida. There Paris was asked to judge the 'fairest' between Hera, Athena and Aphrodite. All were beautiful in their own way, and each offered Paris a bribe in the hope she would be chosen. Hera's bribe was power over all the known world; Athena offered him victory in battle; and Aphrodite promised him the most beautiful woman in the world. Paris was young, handsome and virile, and had no hesitation in handing the golden apple to Aphrodite.

To fulfil her promise, Aphrodite arranged for King Priam to send Paris on a mission to King Menelaus of Sparta. On his arrival he was entertained at a banquet held in his honour at which Menelaus' wife Helen, renowned for being the most beautiful woman in the world, was present. As soon as she and Paris set eyes on each other a flame of passion ignited between them.

While King Menelaus was absent, attending to the funeral arrangements of his grandfather in Crete, Paris persuaded Helen to run away with him. Not only did he steal the king's wife, but he also took a quantity of Spartan treasure. It was an intolerable abuse of King Menelaus' hospitality, a breach of etiquette, a slur on the king's honour. His wife seduced by the King of Troy's son? What an impertinence!

King Menelaus turned to his brother King Agamemnon of Mycenae; family honour had to be restored. The outcome was the long and bloody Trojan War.

CHAPTER

# 1

# MT. IDA

The road we were on was flanked by olive groves, which in turn became forested slopes. We passed a mule being led by a peasant, and we saw a herd of goats. The forest then changed to hummocky hills sparsely covered with fir-trees interspersed with large grey boulders. We must by now be on the lower slopes of Mt. Ida, the mountain where the Judgement of Paris was said to have taken place with the disastrous consequence of the Trojan War. The Judgement, of course, was when Paris, son of King Priam of Troy, was ordered by Zeus, supreme god of all the Olympians, to judge who was the fairest of three goddesses: Athena, goddess of wisdom, arts and crafts; Hera, goddess of women and marriage; and Aphrodite, goddess of love.

"We're now in Judgement territory," I said to Harry, straining my neck as I looked upwards to the mountain peaks.

"Why on earth did the blessed goddesses have to be judged all the way out here and not where the golden apple was thrown down in Greece?" Harry demanded. The long journey was making him irritable.

"Well – " and I explained how the supreme god had obviously known that to give the golden apple to 'the fairest' goddess at the wedding would have caused an uproar amongst the many 'fair ones' who weren't presented with it. And so he'd commanded its removal far away to this mountain.

"One of these wild Greek stories," Harry grumbled. "God knows why I agreed to this trip."

We'd already spent a couple of days in a small seaside town called Ayvalik, an attractive spider's web of a place built on a hillside with narrow cobbled streets rising from its sea-front lined with many restaurants. Turkey's vast landscape required long overland journeys, so on this occasion we were treating ourselves to the simplicity of taxi-transfers from the airport at Izmiz to Ayvalik, and again from there to our new destination on Mt. Ida. Ayvalik had given us a chance to recover from the stresses and strains of being on time for trains and planes. To get anywhere at all abroad always seemed to me a remarkable achievement, and to be here now on the lower slopes of Mt. Ida was a positive triumph.

Our driver was a young man with a neat black beard. He had a habit of leaning on his arm-rest, and absently pulling at the hairs of his beard. When we'd questioned him at the airport about our useless seat-belts which failed to fasten, he'd dismissed our fears with the only two English words he knew 'no problem!' and we hadn't liked to argue.

He now slowed down, then stopped to study a road sign before taking a turning up to the right. We climbed a steep hill and soon saw a signpost with the name of our hotel on it. Through the fir-trees on our left we glimpsed a large, solidly built house set in its own pleasantly landscaped grounds. We had arrived.

A bust of Homer stood prominently beside the hotel entrance, a suitable reminder of why we were there. Turkey claims Homer as its citizen. To them he was born in Izmir (or Smyrna as it had been called before the 1920s). But the Greeks also claim Homer; they say he lived and taught on their Aegean island of Chios. We'd visited the island some years back, where tradition has it he taught and sang his poems, accompanying himself on a lyre, to spellbound audiences at a place called *daskalopetra* (the Teacher's Stone), a short distance from the port.

The manager of our hotel, who acted also as receptionist, spoke good English. We only had a few days there, I told him, and I asked about walks in the area, and about an expedition I understood the hotel organized for visitors to the higher mountain peaks. The manager was eager to please and said he would see what he could do. Tomorrow he would speak to the resident guide.

★

After a leisurely breakfast, and the enjoyment of breathing clear mountain air, we put on our walking boots and followed the direction the manager/receptionist had suggested we take to reach a village.

We followed a footpath through the fir-trees and almost at once came across a tortoise on our track who eyed us warily. Humans would do well to use the tortoise as their role model: to go slowly over grass and pine-needles amongst spring flowers must be very pleasant and unstressful. There was nothing in the world that could make it rush about and become a nervous wreck. No doubt, he was glad when we straightened up from peering at him and continued on our way, leaving him to take his time to cross the path to get to wherever he was heading.

We soon came to a meadow full of wild flowers with a river winding between tall poplars with their silver-grey leaves shimmering in the sunlight. Here there were nightingales singing. We sat ourselves down on the ground amongst the long, plumed grasses and tall white ox-eye daisies, yellow buttercups and purple vetch, and listened to the nightingales.

It was a meadow where imagination could take flight, and I told Harry that it was surely in some such idyllic spot that the Judgement of Paris would have taken place. The goddesses had been asked to disrobe for the Judgement, so the three had stood naked before him. What would Oenone his wife have thought had she seen her husband then!

"A wife? You mean Paris had a wife?" Harry was surprised.

"Yes, he had," I said.

Oenone was the daughter of the river Cybren. Rivers in those distant days were often given semi-divine status – the Scamander rising against Achilles was a prime example. When tranquil and gently flowing they were revered; but when they became raging torrents, bursting their banks and threatening all in their path they were to be greatly feared.

Oenone had been a good wife to the handsome Paris (at that time he was a shepherd) and he must have loved her dearly because it was said he used to carve her name on the bark of poplar trees like the ones around us.

Robert Graves in his *Greek Myths* described how Paris was at first reluctant to judge between the three goddesses, and had wanted to cut the apple up into three segments and present a piece to each goddess, pronouncing each as beautiful as the other. Hermes, who had brought the goddesses from Mt. Pelion, said firmly that it was forbidden, and he must make a choice because it was the will of Zeus. The goddesses tried tempting him with bribes. Aphrodite's proved the most exciting for this handsome Trojan prince-come-shepherd. A romantic, extra-marital affair with the most beautiful woman in the world? What could be more exciting than that after the tedium of endlessly watching a flock of sheep!

The rejected two goddesses were not pleased. Even in the tenth year of the war …*sacred Ilium* (Troy) *was hateful to them and Priam and his people, because of the sin of Paris when he humiliated the two goddesses, choosing the third* (Aphrodite), *who offered him the pleasures and the penalties of lust…* (Iliad Bk24:26-28)

I eyed Harry through the tall plumed grasses to see if he was thinking of the Judgement as I was. But he was merely staring at the river and idly whacking at the grasses with his stick. When I told him that the shepherd Paris could have tended his sheep and done his Judgement in this meadow right here where we were sitting now, he merely said: "How come Paris was a shepherd, I thought he was a prince?" Whack! He was intent on flattening an arc around where he sat.

"He was that also," I said. It was a long story, but we were in no hurry, and I told Harry how it came about that Paris had been abandoned as an infant. He was undoubtedly the son of King Priam of Troy and his wife Hecuba, but Hecuba had had a dream warning her that the child to be born would bring about the downfall of Troy so, as soon as she gave birth, she handed over the infant to a trusted shepherd with instructions to expose him on the mountainside. The shepherd obeyed but, discovering the baby still alive after several days, took him home. There he had grown up into a strikingly handsome and intelligent young man.

"So there you have Paris as a shepherd on Mt. Ida," I said.

"So how did he become a prince again?" Whack! Harry liked to question Greek myths and find fault with them.

Fortunately I knew the answer. "Ah!" I said. "That was because later he entered some contest held by King Priam, and was so successful that the other sons of Priam became wildly jealous, and Paris had to seek sanctuary at the altar of Zeus. There Cassandra, his sister, saw the family likeness and recognized him as her long lost brother. So he was welcomed back into the family."

"Hum." Whack! "They must have forgotten about the dream, then." Whack!

I could hear the murmur of the river as well as the singing of the nightingales. From where I sat amongst the flowers I spotted what I thought was a nightingale flitting through the silver-grey poplar leaves. It had a whitish chest. Again I heard the piercing whistling sound followed by the short chucklings coming from the heights of the poplar branches. A swift movement and the bird was gone before I could point it out to Harry.

When there was no more plumed grass to flatten, Harry said: "Are we moving on?" He planted his stick into the ground and hauled himself to his feet. As we left I noticed a log cabin through the poplars, and thought I could make out a few people on a verandah. Wood smoke was curling up from somewhere nearby.

We headed on for the village we'd been told about. On the way we passed a couple of Turkish peasants seated on a grassy slope keeping watch over three Friesian cows. The woman was wearing typical Turkish harem trousers, a jacket and a head-covering; her husband had on a baseball cap, old jacket and old jeans. Their swarthy faces looked contented and relaxed and we exchanged greetings.

On the outskirts of the village we passed farmsteads where hens were scratching in the dirt. There was a strong smell of cow dung. The houses were square with terra-cotta tiled roofs, but many were dilapidated. A small, domed mosque was at the centre of the village, its elegant minaret rising alongside it.

From the road beside the mosque we leaned on a low parapet wall and gazed out over gently undulating meadows to mountainous hills. In the foreground were well spaced-out trees which we identified as apricot, pear and almond. The heat of the midday sun was cooled by a light breeze.

"There you are! That's where Aphrodite could well have seduced her shepherd Anchises," I said.

"Who the hell's Anchises?" Harry asked.

"Aeneas' father," I said. "You know, Aeneas, the *Aeneid* – Virgil?"

"Oh, him. Couldn't Aphrodite do better than seduce a shepherd?"

"He wasn't just a shepherd," I said. "He was descended from one of the earlier Trojan kings, and just happened to be tending sheep." And I told Harry how Aphrodite, disguising herself as a desirable mortal girl, allowed herself to be seduced by Anchises, the result of which was Aeneas. When she later revealed her immortal identity to Anchises, he feared for his life, but Aphrodite reassured him that no harm would come to him so long as he didn't reveal her true identity to any living mortal. Unfortunately, after drinking too much wine one night, Anchises blurted out his geat conquest, whereupon he was struck by one of Zeus' thunderbolts and made lame, and Aphrodite left him.

Their son, however, grew up on Mt. Ida and was to fight in the Trojan War. With an immortal goddess for a mother, Aeneas was fearless and heroic. In the final hours of Troy, when it was burning and the great walls and citadels were crashing down, Aeneas escaped to the foothills of Mt. Ida with his by then aged and crippled father on his back, together with his young son. In due course he built a ship by felling trees on the mountain, and they sailed away.

The call to prayer from the minaret suddenly deafened us, drowning out all thought; it was a reminder of the one God to be worshipped here today. Pagan gods? Well, they in their time had received worship, and had been known to intervene in answer to the prayers of men. But here today in Turkey it was Allah.

It was early afternoon when we started to walk back again. As we approached the log cabin close to the river with the tall poplars and the nightingales, we found it was a small café, and we stopped there to drink Turkish tea, a strong concoction served in small glasses with lumps of sugar.

"I wonder what old King Priam and his wife thought when Paris returned from Sparta with the beautiful Helen on his arm," Harry mused as he dropped his lump of sugar into his tea. "The king of Sparta's wife, by gum!" He stirred his tea, and gazed into his small glass as though it were a crystal ball.

"He didn't only have Helen but came away with Spartan treasure," I said.

Harry looked up sharply. "Spartan treasure? Well, well!" He tasted the tea, grimaced slightly, and continued stirring. "It was probably why old Priam and his elders were so nice to her – surprising what a little gold can do!" He decided to fish out the remains of the sugar-lump and eat it. "Though in my opinion no wife is worth going to war over. I'm amazed King Mene-thingummy wanted her back again. I'd have demanded the gold! If you'd gone off with a prince and taken the family silver, I'd be furious!" He could have phrased it better, but made it worse by adding: "I mean family silver, once gone, can never be replaced!"

A nightingale burst into song, and I let the matter rest.

★

The driver/guide/wild boar hunter was a well-built man in his forties who exuded confidence and know-how as we rattled and jolted along – it would be a three to four hour expedition by Land Rover into the mountains, we'd been told.

We drove through a village passing several farms; there were a few small tractors on the road, one pulling a trailer, another a plough. There were fields of tomatoes, beans, and potatoes; in one a family was at work planting out leeks, the women wearing their baggy harem trousers with headscarves. We saw sheep grazing, and a few cows out at pasture. The people were very industrious.

We left the village and followed a pot-holed track ascending the wooded mountain slopes. I had said I didn't want to do an expedition to see the wild flowers which was a trip on offer, but wanted to get to the top of one of the Mt. Ida peaks to look at the views around. It had been from Gargarus, the highest peak of Ida that Lord Zeus had watched the ebb and flow of the Trojan War. His usual residence was a golden palace on Mt. Olympus in northern Greece, but he often came to Mt. Ida to follow the war's progress.

Zeus …*harnessed to his chariot his bronze-shod horses, fleet of foot, with flowing manes of gold; and clothed himself in gold; he grasped his whip of gold well-wrought, and mounted his chariot and lashed the horses to get them started. The pair sped off between earth and starry heaven, They brought him to Gargarus, a peak of Mount Ida of the numerous springs, the mother of wild beasts, where he has a precinct and a fragrant altar. There the father of men and gods pulled up his horses, loosed them from the chariot, and cast a thick mist about them; then he sat down on the summit, rejoicing in his glory and looking out over the Trojans and Achaean (Greek) ships…* (Iliad Bk8:41-53)

Our driver negotiated the track which in places looked dangerously narrow where it had been partially washed away in a deluge several days earlier. The trees were a mixture of plane, fir, oak and beech. We were pointed out a species of fir called the Trojan fir which grew only in those parts. It was dark green and had emerald coloured needles at the tips of its numerous branches.

For a while we drove alongside a gulley with a stream cascading over boulders causing shallow waterfalls. The track twisted and turned more frequently as we got higher. Every now and then sapling firs partially blocked our path having been uprooted by rain and the strong winds; but there was nothing the Land Rover couldn't manage and we drove slowly around or over them. There were fewer trees the higher we went. Eventually, after several more hairpin bends, we came out on the summit – one thousand, three hundred metres above sea-level, our guide told us. A concrete building crowned the peak with a Turkish flag flying taut against a strong and bitingly cold north-easterly gale.

So there we were at last on top of the world! Well, on one of the many Mt. Ida summits. We clung to our sun-hats, and our trousers strained against our legs and billowed out backwards.

"So where is Gargarus?" I asked. I wanted to see the highest peak favoured by Lord Zeus for watching the conflict on the plains of Troy. Our guide turned and pointed westwards over the farming lowlands to other mountains where one snowy peak soared higher than the rest.

"That is Gargarus, or Kaz Dagi as it is called today," he said.

"So are we not on Mt. Ida here?" I asked.

"Yes, this is Mt. Ida too. It is a range of mountains," he said, pointing all around.

"How high is that one then?" Harry asked, looking out from under the brim of his hat which he'd crammed down over his brow to prevent losing it to the wind.

"Kaz Dagi is one thousand, seven hundred and seventy-four metres," he said.

"And Troy?" I asked. "Where is that?"

He pointed north-west. "Over there." He too was clinging to his leather hat – a gift from a grateful Frenchman he'd taken wild boar hunting in these mountains.

Zeus from his vantage point could witness everything – which army in this ten-year war was advancing or retreating, which god was giving aid to which side. He could see as far as Mt. Olympus where, to his fury, he spied his wife Hera, and Athena his daughter, about to leave in order to assist the Greeks, defying his express orders forbidding any of his immortal family to take part in the war '*...Or I will take and cast him into gloomy Tartarus, far away, where is the deepest gulf beneath the earth; where are the gate of iron and threshold of bronze, as far beneath Hades as heaven is high above the earth; then shall he know how I am mightiest of all gods...*' (Iliad Bk8:12-17)

Zeus' family, however, had strong characters and minds of their own. Athena and Hera couldn't bear to be inactive when they saw the Greeks in trouble, since they were the two rejected goddesses and hated Paris and the Trojans.

As I grew accustomed to battling with the wind, my numbed brain recalled other highlights from the *Iliad*.

When, at a later stage, the goddess Hera saw the Greeks being driven back to the sea, and the Trojans about to set fire to the ships, she acted in the best way she could. Using her womanly wiles, she adorned herself seductively and, tricking Aphrodite with a false story so that she lent her a love-charm, she came to Zeus on Mt. Ida.

When Zeus, who like Aphrodite at that time supported the Trojans, saw his dear wife appearing at her most alluring and seductive, he was immediately overcome with desire and told her that never had he felt such love, not even – and he proceeded to list half a dozen or so beauties he had seduced in the past – had Harry under such circumstnces done the same, I'd have stalked off into the night. But Hera was clever; she had her ulterior motives and had enlisted Sleep's help. The idea was that after making love, her dear husband would fall into a somnolent stupour thanks to Sleep, and that would leave her and Poseidon, god of the sea, free to support the Greeks without Zeus knowing anything about it.

Hera, therefore, continued to play the coy wife, keeping her dear husband lusting after her; she merely asked for privacy as she didn't want the other gods to witness them.

Zeus assured her that he would draw a golden cloud around them, a cloud so thick that even the sun wouldn't be able to see through. And so her seductive charms worked.

Zeus *...clasped his wife in his arms. And beneath them the divine earth sent up fresh grass, and dewy lotus and crocus, and hyacinth, thick and soft, that raised them from the ground. There they lay hidden by a... golden cloud, from which glistening dew-drops fell...* (Iliad Bk14:347-352)

Early that morning there had been just such a cloud and I hadn't been able to see the fir-trees from our bedroom window. It had turned a shade of gold as the sun had risen, and in due course it had lifted, and the trees had become ghostlike before they became clearly visible again.

Harry, who liked reading about blood and gore and battle scenes, had read the *Iliad* in its entirety before coming out; he'd been in the habit of reading aloud choice pieces giving graphic details regarding a fatally wounded warrior. For example, a heroic Greek named Diomedes was after Dolon, a Trojan, and he: *...struck him in the middle of the neck, rushing on him with the sword, and cut through both the sinews, and his head still speaking met the dust...* (Iliad Bk10:455-458) or another who with his sword slashed his opponent *...in the neck behind the ear and his sword-blade sliced right through. Nothing held but a thin piece of flesh, and from that Lycon's head dangled as he fell to the ground...* (Iliad Bk16:339-342) or *...the spear of bronze went clean through beneath the brain, and shattered his white bones, and his teeth were blown out; both his eyes were filled with blood; and he spurted blood up through his mouth and nostrils* *as he gasped for breath. Then the black cloud of death covered him…* (Iliad Bk16 346-350)

Harry never failed to read aloud these explicit details as he came to them. He was now playing the part of Zeus looking down from Mt. Ida on the blood and gore of battle.

After a while our guide looked at his watch and said it would take some time to get back, and he would like to give us Turkish tea in a coffee-shop. We returned to the warmth of the Land Rover and were soon bumping and jolting back down the track. He told us about the wild boar hunts he conducted in the mountains. This had to be done on a moonlight night. Wild boars had very poor eyesight but an acute sense of smell, he said. You had to be down wind of them so they wouldn't detect you.

"I imagine they'd rip you up the front if you wounded one?" It was Harry speaking. "Two tusks into your guts? Ow!"

Our guide (we never caught his name, so between ourselves we referred to him as Hunter) made a gesture indicating that a wounded boar was deadly. "You have only the one chance! You shoot to kill! He knows nothing!" he added emphatically when I murmured 'poor beast'.

"Do you eat it?" Harry asked.

"We cut off the head with its tusks and give it as a trophy to the man who has killed it," Hunter said. "The body we feed to the dogs."

"What dogs?" I asked.

"The hounds behind the hotel. We use them for hunting lynx."

When we were down from the mountain, Hunter took us to a nearby village and parked beside a coffee-house where numerous village elders sat outside watching the world go by and idly chatting amongst themselves; he greeted some and shook hands with them. Across the road was the village mosque.

I asked him about a large ring he had on his finger, and he told me it had been given him by a Swedish girl he had been fond of a decade or so ago and he still liked to wear it.

"Did you want to marry her?" I hoped I wasn't being too inquisitive. But Hunter answered without hesitation.

"I brought her home to my family, but my mother said I should marry a Turkish girl," he said.

"Do you always do what your mother says?"

"Always," he said emphatically.

"How do young girls meet Turkish men?" I asked him.

He smiled and launched into the niceties of courtship, though whether he was referring to the modern age we weren't altogether sure. "If a man fancies a girl he sees in the market," he said, "then he asks his mother to invite her family to take coffee with them. If the girl gives her admirer..."

His words were drowned suddenly by the call to prayer from the mosque. Hunter looked up in exasperation at this interruption. Interestingly, all the old men crossed the road to the mosque, obedient to the summons to prayer.

"You were saying something about meeting a girl and coffee," I reminded him, when all was quiet again.

"Yes, where was I before that f...ing noise interrupted?" I regarded him with surprise but he was explosive and unrepentant. "It interrupts conversation! It dominates our lives! Religion! Pah!" He lit a cigarette.

"So what about the girl being invited by the young man's family?" I prompted.

"Ah." He inhaled deeply, and settled back in his chair, flicking ash to the ground. "So the girl comes to the man's family and she makes him coffee. If she gives him Turkish coffee with sugar in it, then it means she is interested in him. If the coffee has no sugar it means she will think about it. If he receives his coffee with salt in it then he knows her answer is no."

We laughed. So there was no wild uncontrollable passion there! Just the wordless message to be understood through the Turkish coffee served under parental supervision.

The conversation turned to the fact that it was the centenary of the World War I Gallipoli disaster. Hunter told us that his grandfather had lost several brothers in that war, but their memories lived on in his uncles who'd been named after them.

Harry said that he also had a cousin named after a member of his family killed during the Gallipoli campaign. It dawned on me that there we were drinking Turkish tea and enjoying each other's company despite the bloody battles which had occurred between our two countries.

Hunter read my thoughts. "Men are not enemies because they hate each other. They do not cause wars, it's politicians who do. Politicians, pah!"

"Or men become enemies because of the Helens of Troy?" I suggested.

Hunter eyed me but said nothing, then began idly playing with his mobile. He was soon showing us photos of his wife and son, then a photo of a wild boar he'd killed a month earlier on Mt. Ida. He told us also of the bears on the mountain but, he said, they liked to lie on cool boulders, and were only found in another part of the Mt. Ida range.

"Do you like your work?" I asked.

Hunter's answer was positive. "I never work, I only live," he said. I thought his reply revealed real enthusiasm, and realized that I too, when I was travelling, researching and writing, never worked, I only lived.

★

The hotel had a swimming-pool and, as Harry thought Turkey would be hot in May, he'd brought his bathing things. The hotel manager/receptionist looked sorrowful; the pool hadn't yet been prepared for visitors, he told us. It was still too cold in May.

That evening we sat beside the swimming-pool in the clear evening light with glasses of wine to celebrate our time in Turkey. In fact, the little water which there was in the pool had a winter's worth of algae floating on it. While we pretended to feel warm when, in fact, the evening air was cold, we heard a loud grating bird-like sound, not quite a quacking, coming from among the nearby fir-trees. This was replied to by a gentle sound nearer to us. I investigated amongst the trees but could see no bird. The loud grating sound was repeated, by which time I was back with my glass of wine. Again nothing could be seen. When it came a third time, we saw beside the algae a small froggy head blowing tiny bubbles from its mouth as it responded with a gentle croak.

"Must be a bull-frog calling her," Harry said.

Love amongst aquatic creatures – Paris calling Helen? Venus, the evening star, hung in the clear apricot sky.

I realized with regret, but also some excitement, that if things went according to plan, by this time the next day we would be in Troy (or Troia as it is called today in Turkey). It was amazing how much ground could be covered in just a few days. In the *Iliad* the gods travelled as fast as the speed of thought. We, however, would be doing the journey as fast as the speed of another taxi-transfer.

# THE FOUNDING OF TROY

The founder of Troy was named Ilus, and tradition has it that he'd competed in games and won amongst other things a dappled cow. An oracle then informed him he was to follow the animal and, wherever it lay down, there he was to found a city. After a long trek it finally came to rest on a hill in Asia Minor, not far from Mt. Ida.

To make certain this was where the city was to be, Ilus prayed for a sign, whereupon a wooden image of the goddess Athena (the *palladium*) dropped from the sky in front of his tent. It was all that was needed to persuade Ilus this was the intended site, and he called his city Ilium after himself. Later it became known as Troas after his father Tros, before the world came to know it as Troy.

In his city Ilus built a temple in honour of Athena and, from then on, her *palladium* was housed in it, and it was a firmly held belief that so long as the image remained in her temple, the safety of the city was assured.

King Priam of Troy was Ilus' grandson, and he married Hecuba. It was their son Paris, whose great love-affair with Helen, the king of Sparta's wife, caused the Trojan War. In the tenth year of the war the *palladium* was stolen and with its loss came the destruction of the city.

# CHAPTER 2

# TROY

It was our first evening in Troy, or Hisarlik as the nearby village is now called. We were in a small hotel within easy walking distance of the archaeological site. Our room was on the first floor with a terrace overlooking the main road where tour-buses taking visitors to and from the Trojan site pulled in and disgorged its passengers.

I hadn't wanted to be rushed through anything which was why I'd booked in here for four nights; it would give us time to see Beșik bay where the Greeks had beached their ships, the vast Trojan plain where the battles between the Greeks and Trojans had raged, and the river Scamander which had played its own part in the Trojan War. All these places had to be experienced without hurry; and there was also Gulpinar, an hour's drive away, where it was believed the ancient temple of Apollo Smintheus had once stood, and where the father of King Agamemnon's slave-girl Chryseis had been priest.

Harry had become captivated by the lives of the major heroes of the *Iliad*: Achilles, Patroclus, King Agamemnon, his brother King Menelaus of Sparta, King Nestor of Pylos, Odysseus from the island of Ithaka, and a number of other warriors, not forgetting such Trojans as King Priam, his wife Hecuba, and their two sons Paris and his elder brother Hector. In fact, King Priam had had over fifty sons though Hecuba (no doubt thankfully) had been mother of only ten.

Our hotel was run by three brothers, one of whom had presented himself soon after our arrival because he spoke English and wanted to be helpful. I'd told him all the things I hoped to see and for which we'd need transport – the sea, the river, Gulpinar – and Uncle Adnan (as we'd come to call him) had made a mental note of them all, and told me he'd see what he could do.

Over the course of the four days at Troy we learned to be tolerant of the tour-bus invasions. I'd known that the hotel was on the main route to Troy, and it had been my reason for being there. It was a question of reminding ourselves of the convenience and ignoring the inconvenience it often caused. For example, whenever a coach-load of tourists arrived, they would overrun the restaurant and the hotel staff would be rushed off their feet. At such times we couldn't expect to be served, and we learned to withdraw to our terrace till the stampede was over. The throbbing sound of the tour-bus when its engine was started up as it waited for its passengers to climb back on board, became music to our ears as it signalled we could prepare to go down again for our breakfast, lunch or supper.

Seated there on our terrace with mugs of tea on that first afternoon, I was pleasantly surprised that we'd arrived at all. Two tall plane trees rose up alongside the terrace, and their leaves rustled perpetually in the prevailing wind. The outlook beyond the main road was to the Trojan plain, a patchwork of small rectangular unfenced fields. We were impressed by the number of farmers who passed by on small tractors, returning to the village of Hisarlik after a day out in their fields.

So there we were at our planned destination. I was really looking forward to the following day and our first visit to ancient Troy.

★

Our visit to the archaeological site at Troy, or Ilion (windy Ilion) as it is frequently referred to in the *Iliad*, was a lamentable failure.

I was over-keen to identify the major landmarks from the *Iliad*, and a massive dry-stone wall, which I took to be the Skaian Gate (quite wrongly), conjured up great events which had taken place there.

What couldn't be disputed, however, was that here at Troy Helen had been brought by the besotted Paris. Although his parents might well have ground their teeth in anger, they had accepted it as a *fait accompli*. Helen herself had been sometimes conscience-stricken, but under the influence of remorseless Aphrodite, who never stopped fanning the flames of passion in her, she continued being what she keenly wished she wasn't – an adultress.

In the tenth year of the war (and Homer's epic poem focused only on this final year) it was decided between the two warring factions that a duel would be held between Menelaus and Paris, and the outcome would decide once and for all who should have Helen. One wonders why it hadn't been held in the first year rather than the tenth.

It took place down on the plain outside the city walls but within full view of those gathered on the tower at the Skaian Gate.

Before it began, swift-footed Iris (a messenger goddess) informed Helen of the duel about to take place on her behalf, and told her to come and watch, and Helen found her heart suddenly filled with *...sweet longing for her former husband, and her city and parents. She immediately veiled her face in shining linen, and hurried from her chamber, with tears running down her cheeks; she was not alone but attended by two female servants...* (Iliad Bk3:139-143)

At the Skaian Gate Priam was with the elders of the city. ... *When they saw Helen coming to the tower, they spoke in low voices to each other. 'Who,' they asked, 'can blame the Trojan and Achaian warriors for enduring such hardships for so long for such a woman? To look on her she is the very image of an immortal goddess. Yet even so, lovely as she is, let her sail home and not stay here to vex us and our children after us.'*

*So they spoke, and Priam called to Helen. 'Come here, dear child, and sit before me, so that you may see your former husband and your relatives and friends. I do not blame you at all; no, I blame the gods. It is they who brought this terrible war on us...'* (Iliad Bk3:153-166)

The duel began and, after several unsuccessful lunges by each in turn Menelaus suddenly leaped forward, seized Paris by the helmet and *...swinging him round dragged him towards the Achaean* (Greek) *lines; Paris was strangled by the embroidered strap beneath his soft throat, drawn tight below his chin to hold his helmet. Now would Menelaus have hauled him away and won glory for himself but for the quickness of Aphrodite, ...who saw what was happening and snatched at the leather strap so the helmet came away empty...*

Menelaus *...sprang back again eager to slay him with his bronze spear. But Aphrodite lifted Paris, as easily as a goddess may, and hid him in thick darkness, and set him down in his fragrant perfumed bed-chamber...* (Iliad Bk3:370-382)

Then, rather inappropriately, Aphrodite saw to it that the enamoured pair were soon back in each other's arms, while Menelaus was left down on the plain *...prowling through the army lines like a wild beast, looking for Prince Paris...* (Iliad Bk3:449-450)

"Skaian Gate? Surely the information board would say so if it was?" Harry's comment was sensible, but I could see no mention of the Skaian Gate anywhere, so this massive dry-stone wall beside which we were standing seemed as good a place as any.

The various information boards had coloured lines denoting the different levels which the excavations had revealed, each level, starting from the top downwards (and there were nine of them), representing from more recent to an earlier era B.C. It was hopelessly perplexing. It was generally agreed that the Trojan War level dated approximately 1700-1250 B.C. These were known as the Troy VI excavations and were in shades of pink. However hard we tried to keep our wits about us we remained totally bemused.

Moving on from my wrongly-thought-to-be Skaian Gate we came immediately to a temple of Athena. I was disappointed because it clearly stated it was Roman. I wanted to see the temple of Athena which had existed on the citadel at the time of the *Iliad*. But as I knew it was customary to build a temple in the same spot as one that had for some reason been destroyed either by the enemy or by earthquake, this was the most likely spot for it. There was a nearby water cistern which served the temple and, of course, all places of worship had to have water for purification.

If where we'd been by the massive stone wall had been the Skaian Gate, then it would have been through there that, after the aborted duel, Hector (King Priam's elder son) would have passed in search of his wayward brother Paris (by then in the arms of Helen thanks to Aphrodite's divine intervention).

Hector found his love-lorn brother idly examining his armour with Helen seated nearby with her attendants. He was furious. Why was he there trifling with his beloved Helen while Trojans were dying all around as a result of his wanton behaviour? He should be ashamed of himself. Paris agreed that he was a disgrace, and Helen herself was filled with guilt that there was so much bloodshed because of her.

With the promise from Paris that he would follow as soon as he had put on his armour (no doubt he had removed it for another amorous fling with Helen), Hector quickly retraced his steps to the Skaian Gate where he found his wife Andromache carrying their baby son in her arms. She was in floods of tears, and pleaded with him not to make her a widow and his son an orphan, reminding him that she had already lost her father and seven brothers.

She implored him to stay with her since he was all she had left, but Hector put duty first: ... *'Surely, I take thought for all these things, my wife; but I cannot hide myself away like a coward and refuse to fight. My own soul forbids me since I have always led from the front winning glory...'* (Iliad Bk6:441-443) He reached out to take his son in his arms ... *But the child shrank back with a cry...in dread at the bronze and horse-hair crest that he saw nodding fiercely from the helmet's top...Then he kissed his son...and prayed to Zeus and the other gods...* (Iliad Bk6:468-475)

I thought of this scene for a moment, before returning along the perimeter path to look out over the Trojan plain. From there we had a bird's eye view of the extensive and extraordinarily fertile landscape mapped out with its numerous parcels of land, each in a different shade of colour depending on what was being grown. If I was confusd by the ruins of Troy itself, the Trojan plain was clearly marked with its rectangular fields stretching away to the sea which lay like a blue border along the horizon. It surprised us how the various trees around hadn't become stunted and bent over with the strong, persistently prevailing wind; instead, each tree stood sturdily upright.

Somewhere here would have been a citadel known as Pergamos with a temple of Apollo on it. When the duel between Paris and Menelaus had aborted, thanks to Aphrodite's intervention, the fighting had resumed between the Trojans and the Greeks, and the latter had pushed the Trojans back. ...*This filled Apollo, who was watching from Pergamos – Ilium's highest point – with indignation, and with a shout called to the Trojans: 'Go on, you Trojans,...Their flesh is not of stone or iron; they are unable to resist the penetrating bronze spear when they are hit. Moreover, Achilles, son of Thetis,...is not fighting, but is brooding by the ships in his bitter anger.'...* (more of Achilles' sulking later).

*Thus spoke the dread god from the citadel, while the Greeks were urged on by Athena...who went through the ranks herself and spurred on any she saw slackening...* (Iliad Bk4:508-515)

There was no doubt that if we were to make sense of these ruins we had to return with Uncle Adnan's brother who was a professional guide. I needed to have the important landmarks pointed out to me. To my surprise Harry agreed.

When we got back to our hotel, we found that Uncle Adnan had already fixed up for a driver to take us across the Trojan plain; he would show us the Scamander river, and drive on to Beşik bay. Yes, he would arrange for his brother to guide us around Troy, he said. He would be free to take us there one evening, if that suited us. Perfect.

★

Our driver was a young man with only a few words of English. We were in the hotel mini-bus bumping along a track between the fertile fields of the Trojan plain. We admired the rectangular plots of emerald green pasture, others of lime green maize, and yet others with neat rows of tomatoes, water melon, peppers, barley, and, yes, paddy fields.

"Rice," said the driver pointing.

Harry caught sight of large grey birds flying listlessly and pointed them out to the driver who said 'storks'. I'd never seen storks flying, only standing on nests. In time we discovered that our driver was, in fact, the chef at our hotel. Driving several miles along the track we crossed a bridge spanning a river. "Scamander?" I asked.

"Yes, Scamander," came the reply. But before seeing the Scamander I wanted first to see Beşik bay: it was into that bay that the Greeks had sailed; there that they had secured their ships; there that the story of the Trojan War had begun.

"First sea," I said.

"Sea," repeated the driver.

We drove on for another three or four kilometres while I scanned the flat landscape for signs of the ancient ditch and wall the Greeks had built to defend their beached ships, but I could see no trace or suggestion of wall or ditch.

When everything was beginning to become monotonously repetitive, we came to sand dunes and, cresting these, we at last saw before us the brilliant stretch of sapphire blue sea and a wide curve of white sand. So this was Beşik bay! Here was the long length of shoreline where the Greeks had drawn up their ships, stern first, secured by cables attached to heavy anchor stones; here was where the Greeks had built their huts.

Uncle Adnan had thought the sea would be too cold to swim in, but Harry was not deterred. Zeus, looking down at this moment, might have mistaken the stork-like legs of Harry for the bird itself as he hovered tentatively beside the lapping sea. He put a foot in, then the other – pause. A slow advance with the water rising to his waist, then suddenly white arms and body arching, and the plunge taken, then only the grey head like a seabird moving along the surface of the sea.

It had been here on the seashore that King Agamemnon had poured scorn on Chryses, Apollo's priest, who'd come with ransom money to buy back his daughter Chryseis, now Agamemnon's slave-girl; she'd been captured earlier in a raid on one of the villages.

Agamemnon had refused to give up the girl, and curtly sent the priest packing. The unhappy father departed ... *without speaking a word along the shore of the loud-sounding sea. But when he was at last alone he prayed fervently to...Apollo...* (Iliad Bk1:35-37)

Angry at this mistreatment of his priest, Apollo sent a plague into the Greek camp and many died. Agamemnon's seer Calchas warned that the disease was due to his insulting treatment of Apollo's priest, and advised him to send Chryseis back to her father together with money and presents to pacify the god. Only by doing this could Agamemnon hope to appease Apollo and get the plague lifted.

The king was not accustomed to criticism, or to have his judgement questioned. He did not want to forfeit his slave-girl but knew he had to save his army. In a proud display of arrogance, he demanded Achilles' slave-girl, the beautiful Briseis, as a replacement for the girl he had to forfeit. He had himself given Briseis to Achilles. Irate that the king believed he could do whatever he pleased whenever he wanted Achilles, who had become deeply attached to Briseis, now lay down his arms and refused to take any more part in the Trojan War; from then on he remained resolutely inactive, together with his army of Myrmidons.

He was, in fact, so disconsolate and enraged by the loss of Briseis that he sat down on the seashore and wept. His mother Thetis heard his cries *...as she sat in the sea's depths beside her aged father. She rose speedily from the grey sea* (except today it was sapphire blue) *like a mist, and sat before her weeping son...* (Iliad Bk1:358-361)

When she learned what had happened she agreed to go and supplicate Zeus. She would tell him about the insult to Achilles and his adamant refusal to fight again until Agamemnon returned Briseis. Until the girl had been given back she would persuade Zeus to support the Trojans.

With King Priam's elder son Hector at the head of the Trojan army, and with the power of Zeus' support, the Greeks were driven back to the sea. Hector's sole aim was to set fire to their ships and utterly destroy them. He was heard shouting: ... *'Bring fire! Raise the war-cry! this is the day, worth all the rest, when Zeus allows us to destroy their ships!...' So he spoke, and they fell on the Greeks ever more fiercely. Ajax himself,* (a Greek warrior) *overwhelmed by arrows, withdrew a little and retreated from the afterdeck of the ship to the seven-foot bridge amidships. There then he stood, on the alert; and, when any Trojan came up with a blazing torch, he drove him off from the ships with his spear...* (Iliad Bk15:719-721,727-732)

Patroclus, beloved companion of Achilles, seeing the Greeks in such dire peril, couldn't bear to remain inactive. He implored Achilles to allow him to lead the Myrmidons into battle. Achilles knew he couldn't restrain his friend at this perilous stage, so gave him his armour to trick the Trojans into thinking it was he himself who had returned to the fight.

So Patroclus rallied the Myrmidons ...*His words filled every one of them with daring, and the ranks closed when they heard their lord. Their helmets and their bossed shields were as tightly packed as the blocks of stone that a mason fits together when he is building the wall of a high house to make sure of keeping out the wind. They stood so close together, shield to shield, helmet to helmet, man to man, that when they moved their heads the glittering peaks of their plumed helmets met...And in front of them all Patroclus and Automedon* (Achilles' charioteer who had yoked the two divine horses, Xanthus and Balius, to a chariot) *stood ready for battle, two men united in their resolution to fight in the forefront of the Myrmidons...* (Iliad Bk16:210-220) [P.J. & D.C.H.R.]

Meanwhile, Achilles returned to his hut and poured a libation to Lord Zeus and prayed for his friend's safe return.

When the Trojans saw who they thought was Achilles leading out the Myrmidons they began to panic and ...*fled across the Greek defensive ditch in no semblance of order... Hector's speedy horses carried him off, arms and all, and he left to their fate the men who had become unintentionally ensnared by the ditch. For many a pair of swift war-horses snapped off their shafts at the yoke as they tried to climb the ditch, leaving their master's chariot behind...*

*Men tumbled headlong from their chariots beneath his axles, and their chariots overturned with a crash. But Patroclus was driving an immortal pair, the splendid gift the gods had given Peleus, and they pressed on without a check and cleared the ditch at a single bound in their eagerness to bring him within range of Hector. For it was Hector that he yearned to kill. But Hector had fast horses too, and they carried him away...* (Iliad Bk16:367-372,378-384)

So much terror and tragedy on what today was a tranquil beach! I watched Harry scramble out of shallow water. Soon he was standing and leaning forward shaking water from his hair and wiping drops from his face. He advanced triumphantly across the warm white sand.

"That was good," he said. Death and murderous battles were far from his mind. "There," he said, and slumped down on the sand beside me. I gave him a towel and he wrapped it around his shoulders, his teeth chattering.

My own thoughts were on Patroclus who would have killed Hector had it not been for Apollo who *...stood behind Patroclus...and struck his back and broad shoulders with the flat of his hand, and made his eyes start from his head, and knocked off his helmet which rolled away with a din beneath the hooves of the horses...*

*Patroclus was stunned; his legs refused to carry him; and as he stood there in a daze, a Dardanian* (Trojan)*...came close behind and struck him with a sharp spear midway between the shoulders...* (Iliad Bk16:791-793,806-810)

"Tough!" said Harry when I told him how Patroclus got killed. He was far too elated after his swim to care about who'd killed whom three thousand years ago. He put on his shirt while I continued recalling scenes from the *Iliad*, picking up handfuls of warm sand, and letting it run through my fingers.

"Hector managed to get Achilles' armour from the body of Patroclus, but King Menelaus seized his corpse," I said. "And Menelaus was the one who had to break the news to Achilles," I went on.

"Achilles shouldn't have been such a chump," Harry declared. "Had he been in the British army he'd have been shot at dawn for desertion."

I dropped the subject, and sat silently thinking my own thoughts while Harry got himself dressed. The shock and futility of his friend's death overwhelmed Achilles with guilt and he collapsed with grief here on the shores. Again his mother, Thetis, heard his despairing cries and came up from her cave down under the sea accompanied by her sister Nereids, and they all joined in his lamentations.

"Well, it was all a long time ago," Harry said, when I reminded him of the occasion. He was feeling in his pockets for his watch which he put on.

I recalled how King Agamemnon at last admitted he'd been mistaken in taking Briseis from Achilles and, swallowing his pride, he now backtracked and offered to return her. When Briseis saw Patroclus' body with the fatal wound, she shrieked. Even Achilles' immortal horses, Xanthus and Balius, wept and *...stood motionless in front of their beautiful chariot with their heads bowed to the earth... And hot tears flowed from their eyes to the ground as they mourned in sorrow for their charioteer* (Patroclus), *and their thick manes were soiled as they fell down from the yoke-cushion on both sides of the yoke...* (Iliad Bk17:436-441)

Harry pulled on, not armour such as leg shields, but his trousers, before leaning contendly back on his elbows.

"It's only a story," he said.

I was silent for a while, then said: "That's when Thetis went up to Mt. Olympus to get new armour for Achilles to cheer him up. It was made by the god Hephaestus, a brilliant blacksmith and maker of such things. Do you know, he even made gold robots who fetched and carried for him! The idea of a robot came first with Homer!"

Harry got up and shook the sand from the seat of his trousers. He noticed Chef waiting by his mini-bus, and drew my attention to him.

When we joined him, Chef pointed to a tumulus which was about a hundred metres away. "Up?" he questioned. "You mean climb it?" I asked. He mimed the act of climbing. Well, why not? Tumuli were large grave-mounds, about twenty or thirty metres in height and quite steep; they were visible from afar and marked the site of a hero or V.I.P. It was said that Patroclus' funeral feast had been held there on the beach, that there had been a huge pyre made with logs cut from trees brought down from Mt. Ida, on top of which they laid his body. It had been agreed between Achilles and Patroclus that on their deaths their bones were to be united in one grave-mound. Many believed that this particular tumulus was theirs, but then for long it was generally thought that their grave-mound was on the promontory of Sidgeum about twenty-miles further north from where we were. In Homer's *Odyssey* the shade of Achilles speaking to Odysseus describes such a promontory. But why? Why so far away? Why not here close by where the Greek ships had been drawn up on the sandy beach?

Chef led the way across a grassy meadow and past a shepherd reclining on the ground with his dog beside him and a flock of healthy looking sheep grazing nearby. He spoke to the shepherd who nodded at us as we passed.

We started to climb with Chef beating at the undergrowth and leading the way. It became precipitously steep as we got higher. I made a mental note that it might be more difficult getting down, but we continued climbing. At the top, the wind! The views all around, though, were stupendous.

Looking across the plain, then again towards the sea, I thought how threatened and vulnerable the Greeks must have felt when the Trojans, the night prior to setting fire to the Greek ships, had camped out on the plain and lit numerous camp-fires.... *A thousand fires burned in the plain, and by the side of each sat fifty men in the light of the blaze, And the horses standing by their chariots munched white barley and rye, and waited for dawn to take her golden throne.* (Iliad Bk8:562-565)

Today there were no horses (for which the Trojans were famous) or chariots; any horse-power rested with the tractors at work on the landscape.

There was a pyramid shaped island not far away and I asked Chef if it was Tenedos. Yes, I was told. It was behind that island that the Greeks had hidden, pretending they had given up and sailed for home, a strategy which finally won them the war, but more of that later.

Harry reached the final pinnacle of piled stones on the summit of this tumulus, and pointed out the Hellespont. Gallipoli was over there. So many courageous young men had died in the Gallipoli campaign, so many in the Trojan War.

He turned back to the landscape, and commented how little livestock there was. I found it curious that both the Greeks and the Trojans had been in a position to sacrifice so many animals to the gods. I couldn't believe the Greeks had sailed to Troy with their ships full of stampeding bullocks, sheep, goats – you name it, they had it. And where had all their wine come from – and food, come to that? It seemed that ten years of war hadn't depleted their provisions in any way.

At the funeral of Patroclus many animals had been killed and thrown on his funeral pyre. The mourners *...piled up the wood, and made a pyre a hundred feet this way and that, and on the pyre's top set the corpse, with anguish in their hearts. At the foot of the pyre they flayed and prepared many fat sheep and shambling cattle with crooked horns. The great-hearted Achilles, taking fat from all of them, wrapped the corpse with it from head to foot and heaped the flayed carcasses round Patroclus...* (Iliad Bk23:164-170)

It had been a colossal pyre and the mourners faced a dilemma: it wouldn't catch fire. Achilles prayed to the winds Zephyrus (the west wind) and Boreas (the north wind) *...and promised them rich libations from a golden cup and implored them to come, so that the wood would kindle speedily and the bodies quickly burn. Iris, when she heard his prayer, went swiftly with the message to the Winds. They were feasting all together in the house of the gusty West Wind...* (Iliad Bk23:197-200)

In no time the two winds *...rose with a mighty roar, rolling the clouds before them. And swiftly they came blowing over the sea, and the waves rose beneath their shrill blast; and they came to the deep-soiled land of Troy, and fell upon the funeral pyre, and the fire blazed up with a mighty roar. Howling round the pyre, they helped each other all night long to fan* *the flames; and all night fleet Achilles, holding a two-handled cup, drew wine from a golden bowl, and poured out libations, drenching the earth, and calling on the spirit of hapless Patroclus...* (Iliad Bk23:213-221)

I looked around, surveying the landscape to the seashore where this tragic scene had taken place. Boreas and Zephyrus were still boisterously at work, numbing my brain. The funeral scene faded from my mind as Chef and Harry came down from their pinnacle.

I was very wary of the descent. By some miracle Harry had no fear that his feet might slip from under him when they were almost perpendicular. Chef gave me an arm but I eventually sat down and slithered as though on a toboggan with Chef backing away acting as a brake holding both my arms with great strength.

We returned across the succulent meadow where the sheep were grazing and where the reclining shepherd with his dog beside him waved a languid arm. We were soon in the mini-bus jolting back along the track across the plain.

"Scamander river?" I now asked Chef. "Please can we stop at the Scamander?"

"Scamander. Yes."

After a few kilometres Chef drew up beside a field of maize. He led the way along a track and to my delight I saw the gleam of the Scamander. We walked down to the shores of this wide river whose waters flowed in eddies around and over boulders. The banks were verdant with small trees whose branches overhung the greeny-brown water. There on the shore I found large mussel shells, some open with mother-of-pearl linings to their interiors, and I picked up several to take away as mementoes.

With the death of Patroclus, Achilles' grief brought him back into the war; his fury and anguish knew no bounds as he went into battle to avenge the death of his friend. Hector was his target because he was the one who'd killed him. But he also slaughtered and wounded every Trojan in his path, and the numerous bodies gradually piled up in the Scamander whose waters became red with their blood.

Eventually the river, a living thing, was outraged: *...He stirred up all his lovely streams, made them rise and, roaring like a bull, flung up on dry land the many bodies of Achilles' victims that had choked him, protecting the survivors by hiding them in the large, deep pools along his beautiful course. The waters rose terrifyingly and seethed around Achilles; they beat down on his shield and overwhelmed him. Unable to maintain his footing, he grabbed hold of a full-grown elm. But the tree came out by* *the roots, brought the whole bank away and fell into the river, which it dammed from side to side, clogging the stream with a tangle of branches. Achilles struggled out of the current and in his terror made a dash to reach the plain as fast as he could.*

*But the great god had not done with him yet ...He rose over him in a darkening crest of water. The son of Peleus fled, getting a spear-throw's start by swooping away with the speed of the black eagle, that great hunter which is both the strongest and the fastest thing on wings...* (Iliad Bk21:236-254) [P.J. & D.C.H.R.]

I reminded Harry of this scene in the *Iliad* and he immediately said: "Isn't that when Hera called on her son, Heffy something, to send fire down to dry up the river and so save the situation?"

"Hephaestus," I prompted.

I was surprised that he'd remembered. *...and Hephaestus produced a supernatural conflagration which started on the plain and consumed the bodies of Achilles' many victims...Hephaestus then turned his dazzling flames on the river. The elms, willows and tamarisks caught fire; and the lotus, reeds and galingale that grew in profusion by the lovely stream were burnt. In the very depths of the pools even the eels and fish were tormented by ingenious Hephaestus' torrid blasts and plunged about this way and that in agony along the lovely stream...* (Iliad Bk21:342-355) [P.J. & D.C.H.R.]

The poor river pleaded for mercy. It no longer cared what Achilles did so long as Hephaestus withdrew the fire. Hera quickly intervened again and called to her son to stop the blaze.

Today the river was at peace, and we took off our sandals and rolled up our trousers, and paddled in its clear rippling waters. The willows and alders overhanging its banks grew vigorously. The tranquillity of the Scamander river made it difficult to remember that Achilles was once hell-bent on avenging the death of his beloved friend, and nothing could stop his advance across the plain till he found Hector by the walls of Troy.

The following day Uncle Adnan had arranged for us to go back to the archaeological site, this time with his brother Mutasim who would guide us around the ruins. I hoped that at last we'd be able to picture in our mind's eye the ancient city, the palace, citadel and the all important Skaian Gate.

★

Mutasim drove us from our hotel to the site entrance. When we'd bought our tickets and were inside, he said: "I will first tell you the story," and before I had time to say we already knew it, he'd flicked a switch to his brain and began his tour-guide can-say-it-all-backwards-standing-on-my-head monologue about the whys and wherefores which had brought about the fall of Troy. I wanted to stop him but Harry gave him his full attention and made the right comments, varying his expression from 'How interesting!' to 'Is that really what happened?' 'Oh, yes, the Judgement!'.

When Mutasim had finished he told us to follow him. I longed to break through his I-am-the-tour-guide-so-keep-at-arm's-length armour. We were approaching the massive wall along the perimeter track. "Is that the Skaian Gate?" I asked.

"No," he answered. "This is the South Gate."

"So where is the Skaian?" I asked.

"Be patient, and I will take you to it." And he pointed close by to where there had once been a gate – not the Skaian – but one in which both sides had overlapped so no chariot could pass through.

I gradually broke down his thick tour-guide shell. We stood at a look-out point gazing over the Trojan plain and I asked him where the Scamander and the Simeois rivers met, the latter was another river mentioned in the *Iliad*. He pointed towards a paddy field and said it was there. He also said there was no trace to be found anywhere of the Greek ditch and defence wall, and that it was anyone's guess where Achilles' tomb was. A great deal was guesswork and he spoke about the German self-made millionaire Heinrich Schliemann who, from 1871, began excavations to fulfil his lifelong ambition to discover the city of Troy. Without any proper constructive scientific plan, he'd put his spade into the ground and started to dig a trench, thus destroying much vital evidence. He'd uncovered what he'd believed to be King Priam's treasure and had secretly taken it to Germany. During World War II it had been spirited away to Russia. In truth it was over a thousand years older than the time of King Priam. The Turks were now building a museum in Hisarlik, and hoped that these Schliemann treasures would be returned to Turkey.

"Where did you learn such good English?" I asked.

He smiled, his tour-guide armour at last falling away. "In London," he said. "I was in England four years, and was first a waiter because I needed money, and then studied there."

"Can you tell us which direction Gargarus on Mt. Ida is from here?" I asked. Mutasim pointed south-eastwards. "Over there," he said. In the early evening light we could see the distant shadowy mountains. I liked the thought of Zeus gazing down on Troy from his mountain peak.

Mutasim indicated the different levels, or strata, to be seen from where we were standing dating from 3000 B.C., and pointed to large terra-cotta storage jars on the floor of a house which was on a higher level and, therefore, was dated later than Troy.

The Skaian Gate? I kept repeating until it became a joke.

And so the shadows lengthened as we did our tour of Troy, and Mutasim pointed out the various ways of building a stone wall which represented different epochs, and indicated the small houses in the lower city for the artisans, and on the higher level, larger houses for what might have been King Priam's family – Paris' house maybe, or perhaps King Priam's palace. Nothing was certain, and all demanded that imagination should be used. He also told us that a beautifully constructed paved ramp, which earlier we'd supposed must be Roman, was, in fact, dated to a thousand years before the Trojan War.

Then at last the Skaian Gate. Mutasim pointed to it triumphantly, as though indulging a child with a promised toy.

So much had occurred there. King Priam had been on one of the nearby towers as Achilles, now on the rampage, drove the terrified Trojans back to the city walls.

*...Both Trojans and their horses fell to him alike. And as when smoke rises up to the broad heavens from a blazing town, caused by the wrath of gods, and causing suffering and grief to many, so Achilles brought suffering and grief to the Trojans.* (Iliad Bk21:521-525) [P.J. & D.C.H.R.]

At this point Apollo had intervened and had disguised himself as a Trojan named Agenor. He *...appeared in Achilles' path. Achilles eagerly pursued the god across the wheat-bearing plain, edging him towards the deep-eddying Scamander...Apollo kept a little way ahead, all the time fooling Achilles into thinking he could overtake him...* (Iliad Bk21:601-605)

It was now that King Priam ordered that the gates be opened so that the panic-stricken Trojans *...fleeing in a jostling crowd, entered the town with grateful hearts and filled it as they crowded in...* (Iliad Bk21:606-608)

*...But deadly Fate, for her own evil purposes, bound Hector outside Troy before the Skaian Gate...* (Iliad Bk22:5-6)

When Achilles realized he'd been tricked and made a fool of, he raced back to the city. ... *Old King Priam first saw him speeding across the plain, blazing as the star that is seen in autumn, outshining all the others in the evening sky... On his breast the bronze gleamed as he ran. ... The old man cried aloud and beat upon his head with his hands, raising them on high, and with a cry called aloud beseeching his dear son who was standing before the gates in his determination to fight it out with Achilles...* (Iliad Bk22:25-37)

Hecuba his mother also pleaded with him, but Hector remained rooted where he was, more fearful of being thought a coward by fleeing from Achilles. Shame was the worst thing, glory the best. ... *While Hector stood pondering, Achilles drew near him, looking like the god of war in his flashing helmet...And Hector quaked as he saw him approach...He could no longer endure to stand his ground but left the gate, and fled in fear. But the son of Peleus, darted after him, trusting in his speed. As a falcon on the mountain, the swiftest of winged creatures, swoops after a trembling dove...* (Iliad Bk22:132-141)

Zeus knew that a definitive end to the war had to come, that either Achilles or Hector must die, so he ...*held out his golden scales and, putting sentence of death in either pan, on one side for Achilles, on the other for horse-taming Hector, he raised the balance by the middle of the beam. The beam came down on Hector's side, spelling his doom...* (Iliad Bk22:210-214)

And so Apollo deserted Hector, and Athena herself tricked him by disguising herself as one of Hector's brothers and offering to fight with him.

"Am I right in thinking Apollo had a temple on the citadel near the Skaian Gate?" I asked Mutasim.

"Yes, but nothing has been found," he answered.

I turned back to the view. It was somewhere outside the walls of Troy that Hector had tried to reason with Achilles, saying that whichever one of them was killed the victor must return the body to the dead man's family. But Achilles was too full of rage at Hector having killed his dearest companion to listen, and Athena gave her assistance to Achilles. He ...*poised his long-shadowing spear and hurled. And noble Hector watched it coming and avoided it. With his eye on the weapon he crouched and the bronze spear flew over him. and fixed itself in the ground...* (Iliad Bk22:275-278)

The two warriors faced each other again. Hector was wearing Achilles' armour which he had taken from the body of Patroclus. It completely protected him except for one spot near his throat. ...*As*

*Hector charged him, godlike Achilles drove at this spot with his spear, and the point went right through the tender neck, though the bronze-weighted ashen spear did not cut his windpipe, so he could still speak. Hector fell down in the dust, and noble Achilles exulted over him…* (Iliad Bk22:326-331)

Hector with his last gasp begged him to return his body to his family, but Achilles showed no mercy, so enraged and distraught was he over the death of Patroclus. He stripped Hector's body of his armour, fastened him to the back of his chariot and whipped his horses into a gallop. …*And dust rose around him as he was dragged, and his dark hair flowed loose on either side, and his handsome head was begrimed…*

*When his mother saw what they were doing to her son, she tore her hair, and cast her shining veil from her head and cried aloud with a bitter cry. His father groaned in anguish, the people round them took up the cry of grief and the whole city gave itself up to despair…*(Iliad Bk22:401-410)

Dragging the body several times around the tomb of Patroclus – surely the tomb would be in the vicinity of the Greek ships and could well be the one we'd climbed? – Achilles finally galloped away with it back to his hut beside his ship. Hector's body, however, never became mutilated because Aphrodite …*anointed him with ambrosial oil of roses, so that Achilles should not lacerate him when he dragged him to and fro. Moreover, Phoebus Apollo caused a dark cloud to sink from the sky to the ground and settle on the corpse, covering the area where he lay so the sun's heat would not wither the skin…* (Iliad Bk23:187-192)

Zeus, perceiving the desolation of King Priam at the death of his favourite son, sent a message by way of Iris telling him not to be afraid but to gather together his most valued possessions, to load up a wagon with them and go to Achilles' hut beside the Greek ships to ransom back the body.

… *'I come here not as a messenger of evil, but of hope.* (How Christian that sounds!) *I am the messenger of Zeus who, far off as he is, cares for and pities you. The Olympian orders you to ransom godlike Hector by taking gifts to Achilles which will gladden his heart. You must go alone, and no other Trojan must escort you, except maybe one of the older heralds to drive the mule-cart and bring back to Troy your dead son who was slain by the great Achilles…'* (Iliad Bk24:172-181)

His wife Hecuba was aghast when she found out what Priam planned to do. He was so distraught and fixed in his intention to obey the divine command, that he lashed out furiously at everyone, including Hecuba as she attempted to stop him. In her despair she called out: …*'Are you mad? Where is the wisdom which people from abroad and your own subjects used to praise in you? How can you think to go alone to the Greek ships into the presence of a man who has killed so many of your brave sons?...Once you are in his power, once he sets his eyes on you...he will show you no mercy at all, nor have any respect for your person...'* (Iliad Bk24:201-208)

But King Priam was too distressed to listen, and told her he'd seen Iris, the messenger from Zeus, with his own eyes and nothing and nobody now could stop him going to the Greek camp.

Neither could the king bear the sight of his subjects and he let out a torrent of abuse at them: ... *'Get out of here, you wretches who dishonour and do me shame! Have you not enough mourning of your own to do at home that you come and vex me here...?'* (Iliad Bk24:239-241)

His remaining sons too received the same treatment: ... *'Move you miserable, cowardly children of mine! I only wish you had all been killed beside the ships instead of Hector...be so kind as to get my wagon ready at once and put in everything I need to see me on my way?'*

*So he spoke, and his sons, fearing their father's fury quickly fetched a fine new mule-cart and lashed a wicker basket on it...* (Iliad Bk24:253-254,263-267)

And so King Priam left the city in his horse-drawn chariot, accompanied by a trusted servant in a wagon drawn by mules bearing the treasures for the ransom of Hector's body. They trundled out through the Skaian Gate and reached the ford at the Scamander river. There he was met by a stranger, a young man. This was the god Hermes, sent by Lord Zeus to accompany the king safely through the gates in the Greek defence wall where divine intervention had sent the sentries to sleep. The old king trundled on till he reached the seashore where Hermes, pretending to be one of Achilles' soldiers, took him to the hut and in to Achilles. Hermes then revealed himself to King Priam as the messenger god, and told him what he must do next, and the king obeyed his instructions.

*...Great Priam came in unobserved by them, went up to Achilles, clasped his knees and kissed his hands, the terrible, man-slaying hands that had slain so many of his sons...Achilles was astonished when he saw godlike Priam. and so were all his men...* (Iliad Bk24:476-484)

At the sight of the stricken elderly king, Achilles' heart was softened. ... *Taking the old man's hand, he gently moved him back; and overcome by the memories of their dead they both broke down. Priam, huddled at Achilles' feet, wept bitterly for man-slaying Hector, and Achilles wept for his own father, and then again for Patroclus. The house was filled with the sounds of their lamentation...* (Iliad Bk24:508-513)

Instead of threatening him with death, Achilles felt sudden compassion; he admired his daring in coming to him to plead for his son's body, and invited him to sit and eat at his table.

*...Their thirst and hunger satisfied, Dardanian Priam let his eyes dwell on Achilles and marvelled at how great and handsome he was, for he was like a god to look upon. And Achilles equally marvelled at Priam, admiring his noble face and words...* (Iliad Bk24:629-633)

King Priam finally implored Achilles to grant him nine days of mourning for Hector, then on the tenth to bury him and hold a funeral feast, on the eleventh to build him a grave-mound, and on the twelfth they could start fighting again. Achilles answered him with kindness: *...'All this, venerable Priam, shall be as you wish, for I will hold up the fighting for the time you require.'*

*With that he took the old man by the wrist of his right hand to banish all fear from his heart...*(Iliad Bk24:669-671)

And so the body of Hector was brought back to Troy and, seeing the wagon and Priam returning across the plain to the city, the entire city came out and wept over Hector. Hecuba his mother, Andromache his wife, and even Helen who in tears said she'd never heard a harsh word from Hector despite all the trouble she had caused. The *Iliad* ends with Hector's funeral rites, and a grave-mound built in his honour.

Harry suddenly pointed towards a corner of the Skaian Gate. "An owl," he announced.

Quietly perching on the stones was a small owl. Mutasim glanced at his watch. We realized we had spent much longer with him than the usual guided tour. The owl, symbol of the goddess Athena supporter of the Greeks in the Trojan War, was an appropriate end to this our guided tour of the ancient city of Troy.

It was our last evening in Troy, and we were seated gazing at the gigantic replica of the Wooden Horse. It might have been a Noah's Ark but for its chunky wooden legs and massive neck rising from its body topped with a horse's head. There were four windows along its body and, at a higher level, there were two more. Wooden steps rose from under it for curious visitors to climb into its cavity. Yes, it was tacky, but parents enjoyed taking their children up to hide inside the horse, and we saw happy faces looking out of the windows. The more enterprising ones waved from the topmost two.

The Wooden Horse story was not in Homer's *Iliad*, but graphically described by Virgil in his *Aeneid*. In the tenth year of the war Achilles had been killed by Paris who fired an arrow at his heel*, the one vulnerable spot on his otherwise immortal body.

Harry, who'd been staring at his outstretched legs, suddenly asked: "So what happened to Paris? Did he survive the war?"

"No, he didn't. It's not mentioned in the *Iliad* but he was later wounded and returned to his first wife, Oenone, on Mt. Ida."

Harry turned his head and quizzed me.

"And did she welcome him back with open arms?"

"Well, she wasn't best pleased to see him after ten years of being ditched."

"Um."

"And she refused to help. But when Paris went and died on her she was so upset that she hanged herself."

"So what happened to Helen after Paris died?"

"Helen? Oh, she married again." And I told Harry how, after his death, two other sons of King Priam contested for her hand in marriage. One was called Helenus, who had the gift of foresight, and the other was Deiphobus of whom little is known except that it was he who won her. Helenus, however, was wildly jealous of his brother, so later when Deiphobus was taken prisoner by the Greeks, Helenus turned traitor. Using his foresight, he told the Greeks two things they should do if they were to win the war. First, they must steal the *palladium* from Athena's temple as this would undermine Trojan morale; second, they must build a Wooden Horse.

It was Odysseus (*resourceful Odysseus* as Homer often described him) who undertook the first hazardous task. The *palladium* was the image of the goddess which the Trojans had always believed gave protection to the city. It was over a metre high, and the goddess held a spear in one hand and a distaff and spindle in the other.

Soon after the theft of the *palladium*, Odysseus ordered the building of the Wooden Horse. The gigantic structure allegedly bore the inscription: 'From the Greeks, a thanks offering to Athena', and concealed within its body were the pick of the Greek heroes. The rest of the Greek army then burnt their huts and sailed away in their ships, leaving the Trojans supposing they had returned home.

Thinking the Greek fleet gone for ever, the Trojans flung open their gates in celebration, and swarmed across the plain to Beşik bay

*See Prelude to Chapter 7

where in solitary splendour stood this famous Wooden Horse.

Homer has Menelaus recalling Odysseus' heroism when he and Helen are back in Sparta giving a banquet: '*...never anywhere have I seen so fine a man, so indomitable a man as Odysseus was. What mastery, what heroic mettle he showed us inside the wooden horse! There we all sat, we Argive chieftains, bringing death and doom to men in Troy. There came a moment Helen, when you yourself approached the spot – approached it, doubtless, at the prompting of some divinity who wished to give glory to the Trojans; and Prince Deiphobus had escorted you. Three times you circled that hollow snare and felt all round it, and you called by name all the chieftains of the Danaans, making your voice like the voice of each man's wife in turn. I and the son of Tydeus sat in the midst with great Odysseus and heard your voice ringing clear, and we other two were eager enough to leap up and to issue forth, or else to answer you instantly from within; but Odysseus checked us and thwarted our eagerness...*' (Odyssey Bk4:264-278) [W.S.]

It is the *Aeneid* that tells us how the Trojans were divided as to what to do with the horse: whether to tow it into the city, or to leave it there. Laocoon, a Trojan prince and priest of Apollo, foresaw disaster; he was right to regard it as a dangerous Greek ruse. He thrust a great spear into the wooden frame. But by now it was the immortal will of Zeus that the Greeks would be victorious, and none of the warriors hidden inside the belly of the horse was injured; nobody screamed or shouted or gave the show away; they all kept their nerve. Instead, what followed next struck terror into the Trojans on the beach, and was the result of divine intervention. Two giant sea-serpents swam across the sea from the island of Tenedos *wreathing monstrous coils, and leaving a wake that roared and foamed.* As a spectacle they were terrifying enough, but worse was to come. The serpents seized Laocoon's small sons, twined and tightened their coils around the small bodies and devoured them. They then seized Laocoon and *bound him in the giant spirals of their scaly length* till they'd throttled him – *his shrieks were horrible.* They then slithered up to the temple of Athena on the citadel and disappeared inside behind her statue.

Mutasim, when we'd spoken to him the day before about the truth of the Wooden Horse had shrugged, and said you could believe it or not, it was up to the individual. He then told us there was a theory that it may have been a siege-machine that had battered down the walls of Troy. I liked to think that with divine intervention anything could happen.

For a while we watched some teenagers dress up as Trojan and

Greek warriors and fight it out with replica swords. I said: "It's odd you never hear much about Sinon, the chap who really won the war for the Greeks."

"Sinon? I've heard the name, I think."

"He deserved a V.C. if anyone did. He was a wonderful actor." And I told Harry how Sinon had allowed himself to be shackled and left behind when the Greeks had sailed away. He'd then been discovered hiding in reeds on the plain, and pretended that he'd managed to escape from being a human sacrifice because the Greeks had believed they could only expect a safe passage home if a human sacrifice was offered to Athena. Sinon struck a tragic figure and threw himself on the mercy of the Trojans, and they believed him. As for the Wooden Horse, Sinon said it had been left there as a gift for Athena to compensate for the stealing of her *palladium*. His acting skills had been so impressive that the Trojans accepted his story.

The Greeks had chosen a night when there'd been no moon, so under cover of darkness they'd set sail from Tenedos. Sinon, having been taken inside the city by the Trojans, watched out for a fire-signal from the fleet telling him they were on their way. When it came he removed the bars imprisoning Odysseus and his men, and they leapt out of the Wooden Horse, killed all the sentries, and began setting fire to the city.

In the *Aeneid* Aeneas, son of Aphrodite and the shepherd Anchises, spoke about witnessing the death of King Priam and his family. He knew of a secret access to the palace. There he found King Priam who, despite his age, with trembling hands was fastening on his armour. In the centre of the palace beside a large altar Hecuba and her daughters clung to the statues of the gods.

Their last hope of protection at this altar failed and they were all killed. Aeneas was gripped by a *wild horror* at the sight of such carnage and rushed off to find his wife Creusa, and their small son Iulius. He felt himself to be entirely alone as the fires raged all around. As he raced to find his family he caught sight of Helen and was seized with fury that all the disasters befalling Troy had been because of her. His impulse was to kill her and maybe win glory and renown for righting the evils she had unleashed by her adultery.

But his urge to take revenge was prevented by his mother Aphrodite. She appeared by his side and warned him that he mustn't blame Helen because it was the gods who had brought about this catastrophe. His duty was to save his father, wife and child. In the general clamour and horror of it all Aeneas found his father who refused to leave, and also his wife crying shrilly to take her and their son to die with him.

Divine intervention in the form of an omen suddenly gave them hope when holy fire appeared to play about the forehead of their little boy. They were at first horrified, but Anchises prayed to Zeus who sent a divine sign of a thunder clap on the left, followed by a trailing shooting star which passed over their house and ended on Mt. Ida.

Anchises saw this as a sign that the family must leave. At Aeneas' insistence, his aged father was hoisted on his back, and they fled through the narrow streets avoiding the Greek soldiers who were on the rampage. In the turmoil of it all Aeneas found that Creusa was no longer with them. They were by now out of the city. Terrified at what may have become of his wife, he left his father and son, and hurried back to look for her. He found his house now full of Greek soldiers with the wind rolling *devouring fire high to the roof.*

But his wife had already died and now appeared to him as a spirit, and pleaded with him to leave and not to give in to grief as it was all part of a divine plan, and he must fulfil his destiny.

"Do you believe there is a pre-ordained divine plan?" I asked Harry. "The fact that Aeneas was saved from the conflagration because he was destined to found Rome – well, some sources say that he did?"

"Good God, no. If he founded Rome it was because he remained alive and had the ability."

"Surely some people are born divinely ordained to achieve something great?"

"Of course not. They do something great because they have the know-how for whatever it is," was Harry's immediate response.

"Like Homer having the gift to memorize his epic poems, to sing and play the lyre?" I suggested.

"I suppose so."

"You don't think his talent was God-given?" I turned my head to look at the great God-believer who doubted in things being God-ordained.

"It all boils down to genes," the believer said.

"So it's all biological chance?" I asked. "Just Nature?"

"Um." Harry wasn't going to jeopardise his God-belief by reducing the Almighty to the divine mystery of Nature. God to him was larger than life, greater than Nature – an eternal Being. I, on the other hand, rather liked the fanciful ancient Greek view of the many gods, the various energies that appeared to move people to do this or that. Yes, these immortals had been given human shape and human passions, but at least they were recognizable, like kindly relatives who could help you in a fix if you kept on the right side of them, but could also disinherit you if displeased. Where in Christianity love (absolutely not sex) and compassion were preached, under the Olympians the divine law was hospitality to strangers and the importance of not abusing it. The devastating consequences caused by Paris' abuse whilst a guest at the palace of King Menelaus was a prime example.

We saw Mutasim walking the other side of the Wooden Horse. We knew he had been taking a group of French tourists around the site that afternoon, and I imagined they were now swarming through the hotel and the gift shop. That morning he had taken us to Gulpinar, to the temple of Apollo Smintheus there. I'd read that it had been at this temple that Chryses had been priest. It had been he who'd arrived with ransom money to buy back his daughter Chryseis from King Agamemnon, only to be insulted and sent on his solitary way without her.

A temple had existed at the time of the Trojan War. The story was that during the Bronze Age some Cretans, wanting to settle in the area, had been told by an oracle to found their new settlement wherever they were attacked by the 'earth-born'. They put ashore in the area of Gulpinar and during the night all their leather equipment had been nibbled by mice. This they'd taken to be the sign meant by the oracle. A temple was built on the spot and dedicated to Apollo Smintheus (the mouse god).

The present remains of tall white Roman columns and adjoining ruins were a kilometre or so inland from a deep inlet. From the present temple we'd been able to see the sapphire blue sea beyond a forest of green trees. It has to be remembered that in response to the priest's prayers to Apollo a plague had descended on the Greek army (caused by mice or rats?) and Agamemnon had felt compelled to return Chryseis, the priest's daughter, together with suitable compensation and sacrificial offerings.

While at Gulpinar it had been easy to visualize Odysseus' ship sailing along the coast bringing back the lovely Chryseis. She herself must have been overjoyed as the ship, laden with treasures for her father, had neared her home and she'd glimpsed her father's temple.

*... Odysseus came to Chryse* (Gulpinar) *with the holy offerings. When they had brought their ship into the deep haven, they furled their sails and*

*stowed them in the black ship; and lowered the mast,... and rowed her to her anchorage. Then they cast out mooring-stones and made fast the hawsers, and jumped out on to the beach. The cattle for the Archer-god Apollo were disembarked, and Chryseis stepped ashore... Then Odysseus of many counsels brought her to the altar and gave her into her father's arms and said:*

*'Chryses, Agamemnon king of men sent me to bring you your daughter, and to make a holy offering of oxen to Apollo on the Greeks' behalf, in the hope of pacifying the god who has been inflicting sorrow and mourning on our men.' With these words he gave her to his arms, and he gladly took his dear child...* (Iliad Bk1:431-447)

The small museum there at Gulpinar had been closed that morning. It apparently held panels of a frieze from the temple depicting scenes from the Trojan War, the earliest ever to be found in Anatolia.

Mutasim spotted us on the seat and walked towards us. "Can I join you?" he asked.

"Of course," I said. "You must be tired after driving us this morning and doing a tour of the site with the French this afternoon."

He regarded me with his blue eyes – Uncle Adnan also had blue eyes and told me that it was a feature of those descended from the Trojans. "My wife is always urging me to do less," Mutasim said. "But Troy is my passion. No, I'm not tired."

What he said reminded me of Hunter on Mt. Ida who'd told us that he never worked, he only lived, and I told this to Mutasim.

"Ah! I will repeat that to my wife!" he said. "I am not working, I am living!"

Harry who was still staring at his outstretched legs and tapping his feet with the point of his stick, suddenly asked: "So what happed to Helen when Troy was being destroyed?"

"Ah, that is a good question," Mutasim said. Homer does not give details of the burning of Troy. That was left to later writers and also to artists. It is generally accepted that Menelaus discovered Helen cowering in a corner of a room in the palace of her then husband Deiphobus."

"Her new husband after the death of Paris?" Harry enquired.

"That's right," Mutasim agreed. "The general belief is that on seeing his wife, Menelaus in a blind fury drew his sword intending to kill her, but Aphrodite intervened. Helen is shown by artists standing before her husband, either drawing her veil across her face in an act of modesty, or maybe away from her face to reveal her beauty. Or, as some say, she lowered her garment to reveal her body. Whatever she did Menelaus was again overcome by his love for her and dropped his sword. So they were reconciled."

"It was really very unfair," I remarked. "After being the cause of so many deaths and so much unhappiness, she returned safely to Sparta and lived peacefully into old age with Menelaus."

"Life is unaccountably unfair," Mutasim agreed. "Can I give you a lift back to the hotel?" he asked.

Yes, he could.

Later that evening I asked Mutasim if he was able to play a long-necked mandolin type instrument which was hanging on the restaurant wall. He modestly said he was no good, but would give it a try. He sat with it across his knee and, with a look of fixed concentration began to pluck the strings and produce a steady rhythmic tune. He could have been Homer accompanying himself on the lyre; he just needed to add his voice and start chanting the *Iliad*, its introductory verse, perhaps: *Anger – sing, goddess, the wrath of Achilles son of Peleus, the ruinous wrath, which brought the Greeks endless sufferings, and hurled down into Hades many strong souls of heroes, and gave their bodies to be a prey for dogs and all winged birds; and so the counsel of Zeus was fulfilled from the day Agamemnon king of men and godlike Achilles quarrelled and parted.* (Iliad Bk1:1-6) [P.J. & D.C.H.R.]

DION
LITOCHORO
CHAPTER 8:
MOUNT
OLYMPUS
MT.
OLYMPUS
AEGEAN SEA
GREECE
CHAPTER 7:
MOUNT
PELION
MT.
PELION
VOLOS
DELPHI
ITHAKA
CEPHALONIA
CHAPTER 5:
ITHAKA
MYCENAE
NAUFLIO
CHAPTER 3:
MYCENAE
ARGOLIS GULF
IONIAN
SEA
NESTOR'S
PALACE
ANCIENT
PYLOS
PYLOS
CHAPTER 6:
PYLOS
MYSTRAS
SPARTA
KALAMATA
GYTHION
MANI
CHAPTER 4:
SPARTA
N
W
E
S

# GREECE

# THE CURSE OF THE HOUSE OF ATREUS

Agamemnon and his brother Menelaus were the sons of King Atreus of Mycenae. There was, however, bad blood in the family. It started with their great-grandfather Tantalus who killed his son, stewed up his shoulder, and served it to the gods to see if they could distinguish between human and animal flesh. They certainly could and, for this dastardly act, the gods condemned him for eternity to stand in water up to his neck, unable to quench his thirst because, whenever he leaned forward to drink, the water receded out of his reach.

Pelops, the son whom Tantalus had killed, was restored to life by the gods, and given a new shoulder made of ivory. He later became the father of Atreus and Thyestes, in whom the bad blood continued to manifest itself. Atreus became king of Mycenae and married Aerope who was seduced by Thyestes. On learning about it, Atreus took his revenge by serving up to Thyestes a casserole containing the boiled remains of his two young children. After the meal he told him what he had eaten and, out of sheer spite, showed him their hands and feet. As a result Thyestes fled the kingdom, and brought down a curse on the house of Atreus which was to run through the family for another three generations. Thyestes, with the bad blood in his veins, seduced his own daughter with whom King Atreus later fell in love and, not knowing she was his niece, brought her to the palace. She gave birth to a son, Aegisthus, who was brought up in the palace at Mycenae with Agamemnon and Menelaus.

These unsavoury details of the family's past are important to know as the curse resurfaces throughout the life of Agamemnon.

When Agamemnon grew up he married Clytemnestra, daughter of King Tyndareus of Sparta and his wife Leda; she was sister of the beautiful Helen, and her brothers were the Dioscuri (Castor and Polydeuces). Agamemnon and Clytemnestra had three daughters, and a son. Two of the daughters were Iphigenia and Electra; the former played an important but tragic rôle at the outset of the Trojan War, while Electra suffered the trauma of her father's murder by her mother on his return from the war. As for Orestes, he was doomed to endure a trail of torments which followed on from these events.

# CHAPTER 3 MYCENAE

In order to visit King Agamemnon's palace at Mycenae, as well as other important sites in the vicinity, we based ourselves at Nauflio, an elegant town and port overlooking the Gulf of Argolis.

Nauflio, it is believed, was named after Nafplios, a son of Poseidon. After his death, his son Palamedes became king, and it was he who helped Menelaus get the support of the many kings of Greece to fight the Trojan War.

Early our first morning I sat on our hotel balcony and looked out over the sea-front lined with palm trees, to the small fortified islet of Bourdzi. The sea was a silvery-blue gleam and very still; there was a long jetty at the end of which a harbour light flashed at regular intervals; far beyond was another bay with a tree-fringed shoreline and distant mountains; a few small boats were moving silently on the still waters, and several patient fishermen were on the jetty casting out their lines for an early-morning catch. There was a light coverlet of high cloud veiling the heavens, though through gaps here and there were patches of pale blue sky.

The goddess Hera, consort of Zeus, presided over the region around the ancient city of Argos, some eleven kilometres from Nauflio, and that first morning we paid our respects to her temple known as the *Heraion.*

★

We climbed up to the highest of the three terraces on which successive temples had been built. On this highest level there were massive-girthed Cyclopean boulders from the Mycenaean period.

From up there we were able to gaze across the Argolid plain which stretched beyond the modern town of Argos four kilometres away, to the hazy grey mountains of Arcadia; further south we could glimpse the blue of the Gulf of Argolis.

I was very conscious of the part Hera had played in assisting the Greeks in the Trojan War. Before climbing to this terrace we had first paused by the padlocked metal-meshed gate in the area's perimeter fence, and peered through at a pathway flanked by olive trees which had once been the Sacred Way coming from the palace of Mycenae about three kilometres away. It had been along that Sacred Way that King Agamemnon had walked from his palace accompanied by his nobles who had sworn their allegiance to him before the goddess before setting off for Troy.

One of them must have been the great hero Diomedes, king of Argos. He had accompanied Odysseus on some of his more daring escapades (the stealing of the *palladium* from Athena's temple, for example). His home-coming after the war had not been a happy one, however, because in the war he had attacked Aphrodite's son Aeneas: *...Diomedes grabbed a large boulder which two men together would find hard to carry, yet he with ease wielded it alone. With it he struck Aeneas on the hip, where the thigh turns in the hip-joint – the cup-bone, as they call it. He crushed the cup-bone and he broke both sinews also – and the jagged boulder tore the skin...and the darkness of night veiled his eyes...Seeing what had happened, she* (Aphrodite) *wound her white arms round her dear son, and drew a fold of her radiant robe across him, to protect him from the arrows or any fatal spear thrust in the breast from the Greek charioteers which would take away his life...* (Iliad Bk5:303-318)

In his fury at the disappearance of his quarry Diomedes had unwisely *...pursued Aphrodite through the throng...After a long chase... he caught up with her and leapt to the attack. He pierced the flesh of her soft hand with his sharp spear at the base of the palm...* (Iliad Bk5:334-336)

As a result of this outrage, Aphrodite took her revenge by causing his wife to have an adulterous fling during his absence. Some say that Diomedes was king of Argos by marriage only and that, after his wife left him, the throne was seized by the new legitimate heir. Fleeing for his life Diomedes sought refuge here at Hera's sanctuary, but later went to Italy never to return.

According to tradition, it was here at the *Heraion* that Zeus first set eyes on Hera and fell passionately in love with her. The story goes that he turned himself into a bedraggled cuckoo and Hera placed the creature on her lap, whereupon Zeus turned into the god he was and ravished her. It is said their honeymoon lasted three hundred years.

One of Hera's priestesses had later become the object of Zeus' passion. Her name was Io, and Hera was so angry she turned poor Io into a white heifer to fool her dear husband (though some say it was Zeus who did it to fool Hera). Whoever did what, Hera set a gadfly on the heifer and Io was chased all over the known world, unable to settle anywhere long enough for Zeus to have his way with her.

And there was more to this story. Hera also arranged for a giant herdsman named Argus to watch over the heifer/priestess/Io. Argus had a hundred eyes of which only two closed in sleep at any one time. Zeus, however, was determined to outwit his wife. He ordered his son Hermes to lure the herdsman away from his watch. Hermes thought up the idea of disguising himself as a fellow herdsman and began telling him a string of really boring stories, as well as playing lullabies on his pipes. At last Argus' hundred eyes closed in sleep and Hermes was able to cut off his head. But Io as a heifer was still chased by the gadfly, and it was only when she ended up in Egypt that Zeus managed to turn her back into a woman and she conceived a son by him from whom the royal house of Argos was descended.

By now it was midday and getting hotter by the minute. We sat a while longer, taking in the wide sweep of the Argolid plain before deciding to return to Nauflio to fortify ourselves with food and a siesta before visiting Mycenae.

When we arrived at Mycenae it was late afternoon, and the tourist hoards had disappeared back to their hotels, so there were few people about. We climbed the roadway to the great Lion Gate, the main entrance-way built into Mycenae's massive Cyclopean defence walls. From there a ramp and pathway led on to the palace of King Agamemnon on the summit of the citadel. It must have been under the sculpted pair of lions keeping watch on all who arrived, that King Agamemnon would have passed on his return from the Trojan War more than three thousand years earlier.

"The House of Atreus was under a curse," I reminded Harry.

He turned from admiring the lions and gazed out towards the distant mountain range. "Fantastic views!" he remarked. "Hm, a curse, yes. I forget exactly why?" And I reminded him of the grisly story of the meal of human flesh served up to the gods by Agamemnon's grandfather, and again by his father to his brother because he'd had it off with his wife.

But I was not there to think about the sins of Agamemnon's forebears but to concentrate on the actions of King Agamemnon himself. I wanted to imagine him as commander-in-chief of the Greek army setting off to war to retrieve his brother's beautiful and adulterous wife, and so restore family honour.

The Greek fleet had gathered at Aulis on the east coast of Greece, ready to sail across the Aegean to Troy. Unfortunately, weather conditions at the time had prevented the ships from leaving harbour – some say they were becalmed, others that there were violent storms. King Agamemnon's seer Calchas ... *Who knew both things that are and that should be and that had been before...* (Iliad Bk1:67-68) eventually pronounced that the reason for the adverse weather conditions was, either because King Agamemnon had boasted that he was as good a hunter as Artemis, goddess of hunting and archery, or because he had vowed to sacrifice to the goddess the most beautiful thing in the year his daughter Iphigenia was born, but had failed to do so since it was his daughter who was the most beautiful. Calchas warned Agamemnon that the army would not be able to sail till he had fulfilled his earlier vow. His beloved daughter was by now a young woman.

The king had been grief-stricken, but hardened his heart for the greater good of the cause; he could not fail the army so must appease the anger of the goddess. And so it came about that Iphigenia, passing through this Lion Gate where we now were, left Mycenae having been led to think she was to become the bride of Achilles; her mother Clytemnestra who accompanied her also believed this.

It was with horror that the young daughter and her mother learned the real reason for the summons. Agamemnon performed what he saw to be his duty, and his daughter was gagged, her hands tied as she was lifted onto the altar. Her father was about to cut her throat when at the last moment Artemis saved the girl and substituted a hind. It did the trick and the storms died down, or the wind got up, whichever one was needed, and the army at last set sail for Troy.

Before coming here to the Peloponnese, Harry and I had tried to locate Aulis. We'd driven miles along a motorway heading east (my directions, so it was all my fault). We had crossed a suspension bridge which connected the mainland to the long island of Euboea. Arriving at the town of Chalkis, we'd enquired of many people the whereabouts of Aulis, but nobody had been able to help. I never confessed to Harry that, in fact, we were searching in the wrong place – something I was only to discover later from another map. Instead, we'd persisted with our search. I'd asked a taxi-driver, a shop-keeper, a scholarly-looking pedestrian, but each had stared blankly at me. None had tried harder to discover its whereabouts than a young waiter at a taverna who'd scratched his head and asked a pal, who'd used his mobile to contact his grandmother who, in her turn, wanted to phone a friend... Meanwhile, a leg of lamb being barbecued caught fire and flames shot up to the ceiling. The good-natured waiter excused himself, and quickly doused it with foam from a pressure can.

Aulis? An ancient temple or altar of the goddess Artemis? Nobody knew anything. We'd finally sat at a seaside taverna with a salad lunch looking out over a wide bay. We could see other bays beyond to left and right. Any one of them might have been where the Greek fleet had taken shelter. It was easy to imagine the massed ships unable to set sail because of adverse weather conditions. What did it matter where it was exactly? What mattered was that the armada had finally weighed anchor and left for Troy.

Clytemnestra never forgave her husband for sacrificing their beloved daughter. She returned here to Mycenae where the king's cousin Aegisthus was ruler in the king's absence, and the two became lovers.

We passed under the Lion Gate and continued on to what was known as Grave Circle 'A', an impressive curve of dry-stone wall, built with small oval stones. Heinrich Schliemann had excavated this part of the citadel in 1876 bringing to light fabulous gold treasure from five grave shafts; treasure such as a gold diadem, a two-handled gold cup with small gold doves on the handles, a bronze dagger inlaid with gold depicting a lion hunt, various gold death masks including the famous so-called death mask of Agamemnon. At the time Schliemann thought it was from the body of Agamemnon himself and, no doubt, he was ecstatic. It was later that those with the know-how burst the ecstatic bubble by dating the mask to several hundred years earlier than Agamemnon. A significant find nearby, however, had been a large vase known as the 'Warrior Vase' painted with armed warriors marching off to battle and dated c.1200 B.C. which approximated to the time of the Trojan War. All these pieces we had seen at the start of this trip when we were in Athens and had visited the National Archaeological Museum.

We left the Grave Circle 'A' and came on to the Cult Centre. This was where sacrifices were made and libations poured out to the gods. Well, maybe so, but it was difficult to unravel the numerous ruins in the area. However, with the help of a Guide to Mycenae in my hand we climbed a flight of steps to a spectacular cobbled ramp which dated from the last quarter of the thirteenth century B.C.; it had once been part of the ancient processional way which came from the palace to the Cult Centre. Looking down now over the latter, I tried to imagine the frescoed shrine which had been a feature there, and beyond it a round altar thought to have been the great altar of Mycenae. Several other altars had been brought to light, one of which was horseshoe shaped with a slaughtering stone where the animals had been killed and prepared for sacrifice. A larger building to the south-west of the Cult Centre was believed to have been the house of the high priest.

It was an exciting thought that on the ramp where we now stood King Agamemnon and his family and entourage would have come in order to pay their respects and offer up their prayers with the smoke of the sacrifices to their gods.

Where the ramp petered out we followed a recently made path till we reached the north-western entrance to the palace. So here we were at last, standing before the *megaron*, or great hall of the palace; and there before us was the *domos*, the main room with its large round central hearth over three metres in diameter. The four stone bases which had once supported wooden columns were still to be seen. Before its destruction by fire the walls of the hall had been covered in frescoes depicting warriors, horses and chariots, together with battle scenes. Some pieces had been salvaged and were on show at the museum in Athens.

It was here that King Agamemnon would have sat on his throne to receive dignitaries, kings and ambassadors. It may well have been here that King Agamemnon heard the unwelcome news from his brother that Helen had run off with Paris, and where the decision to go to war had been taken.

Somewhere high up on this massively walled citadel must have been a watch-tower where sentries had stood on the lookout for King Agamemnon's return.

It was sung about by Homer in the *Odyssey*: *...Agamemnon and all his men reached home. In jubilation he set foot in his own country; stooped down to his native soil, kissed it over and over, and dropped many a scalding tear in joy to see his own land again. But a watcher perched above* *had spied him – one whom the treacherous Aegisthus had led to the place and posted there, promising in reward two talents of gold. For a year this man had been keeping guard, lest Agamemnon should pass him unseen...* (Odyssey Bk4:520-528) [W.S.]

King Agamemnon was accompanied by King Priam's daughter Cassandra who, after the fall of Troy, had become his slave and concubine. As a young girl she had been considered a great beauty, and it was said that Apollo had been enamoured of her and, as a token of his affection, he had endowed her with the gift of prophecy. But Cassandra had rejected his advances so, in anger and frustration, he'd brought down on her the misfortune that, although her prophecies would be accurate, no one would believe her.

When Cassandra arrived at the palace with King Agamemnon, she was filled with foreboding. Clytemnestra was informed of her husband's arrival and put on an act of the overjoyed wife but, in reality, she had never forgiven Agamemnon for sacrificing Iphigenia. Besides, she was happy with her paramour Aegisthus.

The unfortunate Cassandra, however, could see much blood and cried out her warnings. She refused to descend from her chariot when invited to by Clytemnestra. Clytemnestra was without compassion and accused her of madness, of suffering from the trauma of having seen her family slaughtered, and her city destroyed.

She was finally obliged to obey the queen's command and entered the palace to face the horror she knew awaited her. The scene of Agamemnon's murder is best described in the *Odyssey*. In the final stages of his ten year journey home from Troy Odysseus was instructed to make his way down to Hades to seek advice on how best to get back to his island of Ithaka. While in Hades the soul of Agamemnon approached him and told him how he had been killed. His story is repeated by Odysseus at a banquet held in his honour by King Alcinous of Phaeacia (believed to be Corfu): *'...I was approached by the soul of Agamemnon son of Atreus...he recognized me, uttered a loud cry and burst into tears, stretching his arms out in my direction in his eagerness to reach me. But this he could not do, for all the strength and vigour had gone for ever from those once supple limbs...'* (Odyssey Bk11:386-394)

Agamemnon goes on to tell Odysseus how he had been murdered. *'"...It was Aegisthus who plotted my destruction and with my accursed wife put me to death. He invited me to the palace, he feasted me, and he killed me as a man fells an ox at its manger. That was my most miserable end. And all around me my companions were cut down in ruthless succession, like white-tusked swine slaughtered in the mansion of some great and wealthy lord, for a wedding...You, Odysseus, have witnessed the deaths of many men in single combat or the thick of battle, but none with such horror as you would have felt had you seen us lying there by the wine-bowl and the laden tables in the hall, while the whole floor swam with our blood. Yet the most pitiable thing of all was the cry I heard from Cassandra, daughter of Priam, whom that foul traitress Clytemnestra murdered at my side. As I lay on the ground, I raised my hands in a dying effort to grip her* (Clytemnestra's) *sword. But the harlot turned her face aside, and had not even the grace, though I was on my way to Hades, to shut my eyes with her hands or to close my mouth...*"' (Odyssey Bk11:404-421)

Here at Mycenae I preferred to think of the king in his heyday, seated on his throne, sceptre in hand, very much in command; a figure of authority.

The views from the palace were astonishing. Wave after wave of distant mountains which in the evening light were shadowed. The Argolid plain stretched away to a barely perceptible strip of sea. Agamemnon and Cassandra might well have returned overland from there by chariot, and entered through the Lion Gate.

We noticed a couple further along on the citadel, one of whom was pointing to the ground at something which made us curious. When we went up we found a tunnel with steps descending to it. Apparently it led to various levels and a well which, according to my Mycenae guide-book, supplied the citadel with water brought by an aqueduct from a source some three hundred and sixty metres away.

We peered over the north face of the citadel and saw it was a sheer precipice where a deep ravine separated Mycenae from a neighbouring mountain. No enemy would have been able to scale this northern face. To the south was a soaring hump of mountain, beyond which would have been the *Heraion* we'd visited that morning. But I could see no sign of the ancient Sacred Way which would have surely skirted around the mountain from below the citadel to Hera's temple near Argos.

I spotted a wild flower growing between two boulders and reached down to pick it, but then stopped. I often liked to take something away with me to remind me of a place, but here I felt whatever I picked would bring with it the curse – a stupid superstious fear, I knew, but it prevented me nevertheless.

"You could take some of those dried grasses back to remind you of Mycenae," Harry remarked, having noticed that I had bent to pick the flower but had straightened up again.

"No, it'll bring bad luck," I said.

Instead of telling me I was a superstitious idiot, Harry rather surprisingly agreed with me, and said: "It's probably just as well. You never know!"

The Curse of the House of Atreus hung all around us like a thunder cloud. No, I would not pick a wild flower from the site, I would be content to take away the memory of it only. My mind was filled with visions of the past. The Trojan War had been remembered down the centuries because its stories had been painted on vases, *amphorai* and clay pots; Homer's epic song about it was later written down for all to read; and the great fifth century B.C. dramatists, Aeschylus, Euripides and Sophocles, wrote plays about it which drew vast audiences.

We walked down to the Tomb of Agamemnon, an impressive beehive tomb set apart from the royal citadel. It was named after Agamemnon because Heinrich Schliemann who had discovered it, believed it was the tomb of the murdered king, though it is also known as the Treasury of Atreus.

Its construction was astonishing with stone-lined walls cut into the hillside flanking the approach to the tomb's great doorway; it had a massive lintel and, above the lintel, a triangular window in its stone facade; the height of the doorway was eighteen feet, and the height within to the highest point of the beehive structure was forty-four feet. It was eerily dark but with a torch we could make out the exquisite stonework to the apex of the roof. Inside there was a second doorway to a rectangular room believed to be the tomb itself, and possibly where the deceased's treasure had been buried with him.

If this was the real tomb of Agamemnon, it would have been here that Orestes, the banished son of Agamemnon, would have come when he returned to avenge his father's murder; and here where he would have cut and left two locks of his hair (one for the gift of life, and one in mourning for his murdered father). According to Aeschylus, the great fifth century B.C. dramatist, in the second play of his trilogy the *Oresteia*, the young man had consulted the Delphic oracle as to what action he should take regarding the murder of his father. The oracle had been clear that it was his duty as the son to avenge his father's murder by taking his mother's life. And so Orestes was caught up in his tragic destiny as the curse on the House of Atreus lived on.

The archaeological site at Mycenae was closing for the night. We had no time left to visit the other beehive tombs named after the family of Agamemnon – the tomb of Clytemnestra, Aegisthus and

Orestes. But since they were only named after them but were not in truth their tombs, it seemed unnecessary.

We were already looking forward to the following day when we planned to visit several other Bronze Age citadels, as well as Epidaurus, the ancient sanctuary of healing. To be able to visit such places and bring to life the Trojan heroes from their prehistoric past was an opportunity I felt lucky to be able to do.

★

We are at Tiryns, a massive ancient citadel which also existed at the time of Mycenae. It has Cyclopean walls, some as thick as twenty-five feet, and the towering mass of it draws the attention and wonder of all who pass by along the nearby road. The views from up here are stupendous with a three hundred and sixty degrees vista around the flat Argolid plain. Tiryns is only a few kilometres from Nauflio, and I've only just read that it once commanded the sea which has since receded. Maybe it was here at Tiryns that Agamemnon disembarked when returning from Troy?

In one legend here was where Heracles was born. Enraged yet again by Zeus' infidelity, and the birth of an outstanding hero in which she'd had no part, Hera wreaked her revenge on this prodigy of a son of Zeus, and by various devices saw to it that he did not inherit the throne. Instead, with her help, it became the realm of King Eurystheus and Heracles became his slave for which he had to perform his twelve 'Labours' which gained him such renown.

There is a sense of majesty atop Tiryns, and in the palace area we imagine a throne, the base of which we'd seen exhibited at the National Archaeological Museum in Athens. Had this throne been sat on by King Eurystheus to whom Heracles had been a slave?

Homer described Tiryns as *well-walled Tiryns*. The city sent a contingent of men who joined others from the locality – eighty ships in all under the overall command of the great but ill-fated Diomedes of Argos.

We drive on to another great Cyclopean walled citadel, ancient Midea. On its summit some of the ruins are thought to have been the site of shrines because many figurines have been found there. Again the views are fantastic across the Argolid plain with camel- and elephant-coloured mountains. To the south-west is a stretch of blue sea.

By the time we visit Epidaurus it is evening.

Epidaurus is the famous sanctuary of Asclepius, god of healing, whose two sons, Machaon and Podalirius, joined the Greek armada with a contingent of thirty ships. Skilled in medicine and surgery, their help had been invaluable during the war. When, for instance, King Menelaus was struck by an arrow, a herald was sent urgently to fetch Machaon, who immediately: *...set off through the throng of the Greek army. When they reached where auburn-haired Menelaus lay wounded, with all the chieftains gathered in a circle round him, Machaon passed through them all, went up to him and drew out the arrow from the clasped belt; but as it was extracted the barbs broke off as the head was drawn out. Then he loosed the glittering belt, the corslet underneath and the apron that the coppersmiths had fashioned. When he saw where the arrow had pierced the flesh, he sucked out the blood and applied soothing ointment...* (Iliad Bk4:209-217)

Later, Machaon himself was wounded in the right shoulder by Paris with a three-barbed arrow. The Greeks were terrified they might lose him. '*...A healer like him, who can cut out arrows and apply soothing herbs, is worth a thousand others...*' was the comment made by the king of Crete. (Iliad Bk11:514-515)

As we cross the entrance to the Epidaurus site, heading for the museum, we are startled by a loud honk, and a police car shoots by followed by two dark-windowed limousines with another police car bringing up the rear. We watch as the fleet of cars stop, and out of the dark-windowed vehicles step a couple of women in evening dress, and two dapper grey-haired men in suits. After they've been escorted in the direction of the theatre, I ask one of the policemen who they are? He is cautious and says they are of no importance; the president of some insignificant European country with his wife and friends, is how he describes them.

Whoever they are, when we come out of the museum building (and we've been there no more than ten minutes) there is another honk and the police cars and limousines sweep away again.

Oh, how limiting it must be to be a V.I.P., even one of no consequence! To be committed to be here or there at some specific moment? To have body-guards watching your every move? How wonderful it is for us to be able to do as we please when we please; to have time to soak up the ambience of a place! Better still, to make fools of ourselves as I am about to do without hitting the headlines in the papers!

The Epidaurus open-air theatre with its remarkable acoustics is world famous, and still draws crowds at its summer festival of music and drama.

We head straight for the great theatre which is resplendent in the evening light. We climb to one of the upper tiers and watch as a few visitors stand centre stage and sing; one or two have good voices, while others start an aria or a song and retire shame-facedly to hide amongst their friends again. It is pleasant just relaxing and taking it all in.

I try to imagine Aeschylus' *Oresteia* trilogy being performed down there. The London National Theatre put on a performance of it here in 1982 with the cast wearing masks as they had in the fifth century B.C. I wish I'd known at the time and been out here to see it.

I am secretly wanting to go down and perform on that small central marble circle, the ancient altar of Dionysos, god of drama and of wine. I find myself talking to a young Spanish woman seated close by. She speaks very good English having spent the last ten years in London. It turns out that we both have the same longing to perform. We are caught up in each other's enthusiasm, but what to sing? She decides on a Frank Sinatra song: 'I did it my way'.

We have a short rehearsal then, much to Harry's acute embarrassment, we descend to the small marble altar. We are intent on putting on as good a performance as possible, though my voice is nothing to speak of.

The small gathering seated in the tiered seats are waiting. Oh, dear! But we are determined to see it through. My Spanish friend is young and beautiful with wavy, raven-black hair, and she wears dark-glasses. She gives the note, raises her hand and sets the beat, and so we start. 'La, la, la, la, la, la, la, la ----.' We are caught up in the moment, my eyes on hers behind her dark-glasses. We reach the final line, the only words of which we know, and sing triumphantly: 'I did it my ------ way.'

"One more time!" she says in the faintest of whispers – the acoustics of this theatre are so good, that her words will have reached the highest seats. We repeat our 'La, la, la, la---s' and with the same flourishing gestures go for the grand finale: 'I did it my ------- way!' We take our bows to a ripple of applause.

It may not have been of a London National Theatre standard; nor, I hope, was it as Harry says with a sort of smile, Cassandra wailing her forebodings as she was about to be murdered at Mycenae.

It is now the end of our Mycenae trip following in the footsteps of King Agamemnon and his family. On our way back to Nauflio, I quiz

Harry about wailing like Cassandra. He takes my hand reassuringly, and says: "Just joking. You weren't at all bad really," which, in Harry-speak is high praise indeed.

Anyway, whatever his private thoughts, nothing will ever take away the ecstatic triumph I feel at having performed where once the ancients had. As the Spanish girl told me, there are magical moments in life, and singing at Epidaurus was one of them.

# HELEN OF SPARTA

Helen's mortal parents were King Tyndareus of Sparta and his wife Leda. Helen, however, was also said to be the daughter of Zeus. The story goes that Zeus loved Leda and turned himself into a swan for his love-making. Helen's beauty was renowned, and her skin was said to be white as a swan.

To win Helen's hand Tyndareus first held a contest to which all the eligible young nobles and princes from around Greece came. They had to display their skill in such things as wrestling and athletics, and to exhibit exceptional strength and endurance in various competitions. Menelaus must have shown outstanding ability to have become the successful contender. Tyndareus, however, had made a condition of entry: all the would-be suitors had first to swear an oath that they would support and give assistance to the lucky winner if it was ever needed.

Menelaus and Helen lived as a happily married couple and had a daughter Hermione. All was as it should be till the arrival of Paris, brought to the shores by Aphrodite after his Judgement when she'd promised him the most beautiful woman in the world. The result was their unconquerable passion and the Trojan War.

# CHAPTER 4

# SPARTA

For this trip I wanted to see where Helen had been born, where she'd grown up and married, where her adulterous affair had ignited, and where she'd finally returned and died. We flew to Kalamata and hired a car. We didn't want to stay in the town of Sparta itself as its later history of a rigid military regime, conjured up visions of a barracks of a town. Instead, we stayed about eight kilometres west of Sparta at the small town of Mystras. Our hotel was close to the medieval Mystras, a fortified city built on a breakaway peak of the Taygetos mountain massif.

Walking up behind the town on our first evening, this splinter of a mountain was silhouetted against the evening sky crowned by its citadel. The grey stone buildings of monasteries, and ruined houses were visible against the wooded hillside with dark green cypresses rising vertically here and there.

We ought, of course, to visit Mystras; anyone staying in the vicinity should find the time for it. But over the days spent there we viewed it practically from every angle, drove around it, saw it from below, viewed it from above, but never actually went inside its ancient walls. It was enough for me that its Frankish founder, William II of Villehardouin, married a woman who was said to have been as beautiful as Helen. That was all about Mystras which lit a small flame for me.

From a road above the modern town of Mystras that first evening, we looked out over the extensive flat plain before us where the white houses of Sparta lay spreadeagled; beyond was the Taygetos mountain range, the sun's last rays of light illuminating its peaks. I searched to the east of Sparta for the hill of Therapne on which the Menelaion, the tomb of Helen and Menelaus was, but I could see nothing from that distance. The plan was to visit it next day, and my expectations were high.

★

The modern town of Sparta as we drove through it was, in fact, quite pleasant; but the town itself wasn't on our agenda. We came out on the main Sparta-Tripoli road along which we drove for several kilometres till we saw the signpost saying Menelaion. We drove up a dirt-track, passing a chapel on our left before leaving the car and continuing on foot.

This was the hill of Therapne and, as we got higher, the massive Cyclopean stone blocks around the Menelaion's flat-topped grassy mound were seen rising from the summit. A strong and coldish wind buffeted us. It was late spring but, thanks to modern technology, we'd discovered before leaving England that the weather in Sparta was going to be cold and wet, so we'd come prepared with anoraks and jerseys.

The track we were on was flanked by tall waving dried grasses, cushions of bright coloured wild flowers, and tall fennel. There were storm clouds around but, for the time being, the sun shone. Occasionally the aroma of wild thyme and sage wafted to us on the air.

And here we are now standing on the Menelaion itself!

The views around are stupendous – modern Sparta lies to the south-west, and a plain filled with orange groves extends southwards to the mountains. To the north is the Arcadian massif meeting the Parnon range; their foothills are terraced revealing ginger coloured, fertile soil. I turn to the east and, yes, far below through trees, I spot the gleam and sparkle of the meandering Eurotas river. The Eurotas played an important part in Helen's life and, weather permitting, we plan to have a picnic down there later.

The Menelaion has a rectangular stylobate, a stepped structure made out of massive stone blocks. It is considered at one time to have been a temple of the king himself where young men came to pray for courage and victory in war. There is speculation that the hill of Therapne was the site of the ancient Spartan palace, but that it fell prey to land erosion and has long since gone; the ruined walls of buildings criss-crossing a lower terrace west of the Menelaion are all that remain of the ancient city.

Massive dark clouds are rolling over the mountains to the south looking increasingly ominous. But never mind the weather and the threat of rain! While we are here I must concentrate on the drama that took place in antiquity. It is of much greater interest that it was here King Menelaus welcomed Prince Paris of Troy when he arrived as the envoy of his father (under the guiding hand of Aphrodite); and here that, at a great banquet given in his honour, the dashing young prince and the King of Sparta's wife, the beautiful Helen, first set eyes on each other and an uncontrollable passion was ignited between them.

In the days when it was easier to sail by sea than to go overland, Paris might well have stepped ashore down there having sailed across the Aegean and up the Eurotas estuary to Sparta.

I try to imagine the pageantry and pomp. Certainly a banquet would be held in his honour, and the royal visitor made welcome. Homer describes how one of King Priam's elders told Helen how he had once played host to Menelaus in Troy who at the time was accompanied by Odysseus: '*...I gave them entertainment and welcomed them into my halls, and I learned much about them both and the way they thought. In assembly with the Trojans, when they all stood up, Menelaus with his broad shoulders surpassed them all; but Odysseus was the more imposing of the two when both were seated. When their turn came to express their views in public, Menelaus spoke fluently, not at great length but very clearly, being a man of few words who kept to the point, though he was the younger of the two...*' (Iliad Bk3:208-216)

Homer often described Menelaus as being auburn-haired. He sang about Menelaus' leadership when the Greek armada was waiting to set sail from Aulis: *...And of them that possessed Lacedaemon lying low amid the rifted hills...Menelaus of the loud war-cry, leader of sixty ships... marched among them, confident and eager, urging his men to battle; for he was determined to take revenge for all the suffering that Helen had caused them...* (Iliad Bk2:582-591)

Harry makes an announcement which reflects my thoughts: "It must have been hellish for poor Menelaus leading his men who all knew he'd been made a fool of by his wife."

"He should never have left them alone together and gone off to Crete to arrange his grandfather's funeral," I say.

"It's not much of a marriage if you can't trust your wife," Harry remarks.

"If I was the most beautiful woman in the world, would you leave me alone for several days, meaning nights, with a handsome young prince? I would say it was asking for trouble." I ignore Harry's surprised look.

We are standing on the top of the Menelaion in the teeth of the gale and I'm aware of the importance of this moment when, as living conscious beings, we are actually here atop the tomb of the royal couple who lived such turbulent lives. By some miracle they both survived the traumas of Helen's adultery and the horrors of the ten-year war, and returned unscathed to live peacefully until their deaths – united in this tomb.

All around us are numerous wild flowers. There are small purple star-like flowers of a low-growing plant whose leaves when crushed smell of a herb we can't identify; and there are different species of euphorbia, vetch, and rock plants, and the list goes on. I also discover a minute ladybird on the furry end of a long stalk of grass; we ponder whether ladybirds hatch from eggs and grow to maturity, or whether this tiny creature is a special species. I learn later it is a species in its own right known as a ladybird beetle or bug; we watch as it separates its shiny, spotted wings along its tiny back as though preparing to fly, and then closes them and remains on the grass-head.

There is nobody else here at this wind-swept site, open at all points of the compass to the elements. We take shelter under a nearby pine tree as the dark clouds release a sudden downpour. It doesn't last long, and we watch the clouds unravel, the dark ones blowing on revealing the colossal grey-white slower moving ones above; these gradually separate enough to reveal patches of blue sky.

We return to the Menelaion because it is unique and we are in no hurry to move on. My mind goes back to the time when the young man Telemachus, the son of Odysseus, came here to the palace to enquire of Menelaus if he knew what had become of his father. He'd been an infant-in-arms at the start of the ten-year Trojan War, and another ten years had passed and his father still had not returned home. He had journeyed here from Pylos where he had first asked King Nestor whether his father was still alive or not.

In Homer's *Odyssey* Telemachus, accompanied by Peisistratus, a son of King Nestor, arrived here at the palace to find a great celebration underway. A banquet was being held for the engagement of Hermione (the daughter of Helen and Menelaus) and Neoptolemus, Achilles' son: *...guests were feasting in the great lofty hall, neighbours and clansmen of glorious Menelaus; they were making merry, and in their midst an inspired bard was singing to the lyre, while a pair of tumblers along the line of guests twisted and twirled to the rhythms of the singer...* (Odyssey Bk4:14-18) [W.S.]

Telemachus and his friend ...*were filled with wonder at what they saw in the monarch's house; for a radiance like that of sun or moon filled the high halls of King Menelaus...* (Odyssey Bk4:42-44) [W.S.] As Telemachus himself whispered to his companion: '...*these echoing halls are bright with the glittering of bronze and gold and amber and silver and ivory. The inner courts of Olympian Zeus must surely be like this house, so numberless are the splendours of it; awe comes over me as I look.*' (Odyssey Bk4:65-68) [W.S.]

During the course of the banquet Helen and Menelaus spoke with astonishment about how much Telemachus resembled his father both in looks and bearing. Telemachus, a sensitive young man, was overcome with emotion and tried unsuccessfully to hide his tears with his cloak, something which did not go unnoticed by the queen. She, fearing a pall of misery falling over the banqueters, slipped an elexir into the wine to keep them all cheerful. She then spoke at length about the courage and heroism of Odysseus, and how she had come across him in the war on one of his more daring exploits (most probably when he stole the *palladium*).

'...*He disfigured himself with ignominious stripes, threw dismal wrappings over his shoulders, and in servile shape passed into the city of the Trojans. They did not heed him; I alone knew him for what he was; I began to probe him, and he to evade me with his cunning; but when I went on to bathe him and anoint him, when I gave him clothes and swore a great oath that I would not tell of his presence in the city before he was back among his own huts and ships, then at last he disclosed to me the whole design of the Achaeans...but my own heart was filled with joy, because my desire had turned by now to going back home again, and I wept, too late, for the blindness that Aphrodite sent me when she made me go there, away from my own dear land, and let me forsake my daughter and bridal room and a husband who fell short in nothing, whether in mind or in outward form.*'... (Odyssey Bk4:243-259) [W.S.]

I think how the landscape reflects the dramatic, spectacular story of Helen and Paris; it is a landscape of extremes – of highs and lows, of peace and turmoil, of darkness and brilliance.

But, as ever, we must move on. As I say a silent farewell to the Menelaion, I feel extraordinarily privileged to have seen it; to have stood on the site while recalling the greatest and most dramatic story of all time. But it isn't quite over yet; we are about to drive down to the river.

★

We are standing beside the river Eurotas which is quite shallow with no banks to speak of; the river meanders between what are really only banked up off-white pebbles of various sizes from which a few plants here and there struggle up in tufts. We have just broken cover having walked from the road along a path flanked by rustling bamboos, willows, alders and plane trees. As we emerge at the river's edge we startle a couple of white egrets which skim off upriver and come to rest at a bend where they keep watch on us intruders. The water glitters darkly, reflecting the ominous clouds. Beyond the river the wide fertile Spartan plain stretches to the distant mountain ranges.

I wonder if Helen ever knew her father was a swan, or rather that Zeus took the form of a swan to ravish her mother, and I put the question to Harry.

He picks up a round flat pebble and skims it across the surface of the river; it skips three times.

"Or, for that matter, that she was hatched from an egg," I say. "I'd feel very mixed-up if I learned that my father was a god who'd had it off with my mother disguised as a swan."

Harry picks up another flat pebble. "Why Zeus wanted to be a bird beats me. Why not just be himself?" he says, and tries another skimming-of-the-water with his pebble, but it only skips twice.

The travel-writer Pausanias of the second century A.D. mentioned the large egg-shell from which Helen was thought to have been hatched. Legend has it that the egg was laid (presumably by Leda) and left somewhere on the river bank, no doubt close to where we are standing not far from the palace.

The mountain peaks by now are hidden in storm clouds, and we can see a sheet of slanting rain descending from them. The river has a certain magical quality about it, and flows gracefully like the curving neck of a swan along the wide stretch of fertile landscape of orange groves.

We sit on a pebbly mound and watch the flowing water while we eat our sandwiches. Although it isn't the most beautiful landscape, there is a quiet magic about it; maybe it's the mind's eye working on the story of the young Helen. Close by where we sit some unidentified and rooted water plant is streaming out like seaweed with small white daisy-like flowers.

Apparently, from the eighth century B.C. (and Helen lived much earlier, c.1250 B.C.) the memory of Helen took on a divine role and she was evoked as a goddess at numerous cult shrines. Valuable objects have been found dedicated to her. The fifth century B.C. historian Herodotus described how it became the custom for anyone seeking beauty to come to her temple on the hill of Therapne. He wrote how a nurse, whose charge had been a baby girl (regretfully quite hideous) had taken the infant daily to a temple to beseech Helen to bestow beauty on the child. One day a woman appeared to the nurse and insisted on seeing the baby she was carrying in her arms. She stroked the ugly head and assured the nurse the child would become a beauty. From then on her ugliness faded and she grew up to be so lovely that the then King of Sparta was captivated by her looks and married her.

We are unable to entice the egrets back to us, and it begins to spit with rain. We have finished our picnic, but I'm in no hurry to go back to the car. Instead, I lead the way along a fork in the track which takes us further down river through the tall bamboos whose numerous thin leaves rustle in the wind. Two birds are startled and take flight; they look like partridges but their fanned out tails are edged with white. Harry wonders if they are quails.

There is an unpleasant story regarding Helen which I do not mention to Harry because it can only mar the tranquillity of our surroundings. One day Theseus, the aging King of Athens, spied the beautiful Helen when she was still a young child, bathing naked with her playmates in this river. He might well have been lurking amongst such bamboos and trees that we are passing through. Overcome by desire, and used to getting his own way, he seized and raped her. The story casts a shadow over the other Theseus tales which are romantic or heroic and cling more attractively to his memory.

So, not only was Helen raped as a child, but to all extents and purposes she was born of a rape also. But whatever her misfortunes, down the centuries and the millennia, her beauty and aura and charisma remain unblemished in the human mind. Our word 'charisma' comes from the ancient Greek *charis* meaning 'grace', 'loveliness'. No matter how many strange, even horrific stories surround Helen, the overall image of her somehow remains untouched. As the ideal of untarnished beauty she retains her perfection. Yes, she had human frailties; yes, she caused abject misery and distress, but her femininity and beauty have never diminished.

It is now raining more heavily so we return to the car. Tomorrow we plan to drive down south into the Mani region. We'll be heading for a small islet where the love-struck Helen and Paris are said to have spent their first night together. I feel it an honour to be following in the footsteps of the most beautiful woman in the world.

★

The Maniots are descended from the ancient Spartans with a mix of Slavonic blood. They were notorious for their ferocious family feuds and vendettas, and their houses are famous for their square towers, from which they could keep watch against approaching enemies.

On the way south I knew we would be passing close to the ancient settlement of Amyklae where there had once been a sanctuary of Apollo. It was there that it was thought the contest held by Tyndareus for his daughter Helen's hand in marriage had been held. It was also believed that Helen had been worshipped at the sanctuary, and a festival known as the *Heleneia* had been celebrated.

The sanctuary was where tradition has it Apollo became besotted by a handsome youth named Hyakinthus. The grandfather of Hyakinthus was Lacedaemon and his mother was named Sparte (after both of whom the Lacedaemons of Laconia were called, and the town of Sparta). Tragically, Apollo accidentally killed his beloved Hyakinthus while they were practising discus-throwing. In fact, it was said that Zephyrus, the west wind, who also loved the youth and was angry and jealous of Apollo's devotion to him, deliberately blew the discus off course so that it hit Hyakinthus on the head and killed him. Apollo was distraught and turned the young man's blood into a form of hyacinth (some say it was a short, purple iris).

The tomb of Hyakinthus was thought to be within the sanctuary of Apollo, and in the sanctuary there had been a great statue of Apollo seated on a throne of gold and ivory. A festival known as the *Hyakinthia* was held annually in July in honour of Apollo's favourite.

Having taken a wrong turning to Amyklae, we asked some workmen, one of whom immediately hopped into his car and told us to follow him, apparently happy to skive off work for ten minutes. He led us to this gently undulating site with a low mound topped by the chapel of Agia Kyriaki, said to stand on the site of Apollo's statue.

The sanctuary was surrounded by a wire-mesh fence with a padlocked door. We could see sheets of black plastic weighed down by large stones, covering an area which we presumed were newly dug excavations. There were several old eucalyptus trees whose silvery flaking brown trunks towered skywards and whose pendulous branches with their numerous narrow leaves drooped earthwards. Below and beyond the slight rise in the landscape, orange and olive groves as ever stretched away to the mountains. A CCTV camera kept watch, not so much over the archaeological site at Amyklae, but on a strong metal, barred gate and entrance to a large private estate.

We were glad to have seen the site, but we were soon on our way again to Gythion, the road to which was flanked by woods which in turn gave way to olive groves, then more tall eucalyptus. We headed south for about thirty kilometres before taking a left turn to Gythion, the ancient port, which today is an attractive array of houses with terra-cotta roofs surrounding a wide bay of silver-blue sea.

The purpose here was to visit the small islet of Kranae as Homer called it (meaning 'rocky') where Helen and Paris spent their first rapturous night together. Today the islet is known as Marathonisi ('fennel island') and is connected to the mainland by a causeway. We cautiously drove along the causeway and managed to park conveniently under a tall, shady pine tree.

A Mani-type building on the islet turned out to be a small museum. There was also a terra-cotta domed whitewashed church, as well as a fenced-off lighthouse perched on the far extremity of the islet. A gleaming white four-masted schooner was anchored offshore at the eastern end of the bay looking majestic against the coastline.

A couple of weary looking elderly Americans ambled past us grumbling. "To bring us here, then to find it locked. You'd think they'd unlock the church for us! I can't see what's special about this place. Why bring us here?"

"I seem to recall the guide saying something about Helen."

"Helen who?"

"I'm thinking maybe she's the mother of Constantine."

"Helen of Troy," I prompted. I couldn't stay silent on what to me was such a major subject.

"You don't say!" said the woman, turning towards me in some surprise.

"Helen of Troy?" echoed the man. "Did she come from around these parts, then?" Helen clearly wasn't important to them.

"From Sparta," said Harry with a spark of enthusiasm. He normally never speaks to strangers, but his bit of information came out with his breath.

"Are you on a tour?" I asked.

"We're off that yacht you see there," said the woman. "We boarded in Rome, and called in at Athens. I don't know why they've brought us here, though. Why not take us straight to Mystras."

"They say Mystras is quite something," said the man. I expect this lady and gentleman have been to Mystras?" he questioned.

We admitted we had seen it only from the distance, and their expressions changed revealing that they thought us abysmal failures.

Another couple approached and the woman continued to grumble. "All this way and the church is locked, Lucille. You'd have thought they'd unlock it for us." And the four groused away together about the cold wind, the clouds and impending rain.

But for the time being the sun was out. We crept over the rocks which fringed the islet. It was like pumice-stone, eroded and contorted with numerous cavities and holes. Despite that, tufts and cushions of wild flowers had rooted themselves. The first night for the lovers must surely have been on a bed of wild flowers, under a starry sky and a full moon? Aphrodite would not have failed to have spun beauty and enchantment around the amorous pair. Before the causeway linked Kranae to the mainland, Kranae would have been an isolated paradise lapped by the sea.

Somewhere along the coast across the bay must be the estuary to the river Eurotas. Had Paris sailed with Helen down-river to the Laconian gulf here? And from here had he taken her to Troy? Or was the story altogether different? According to the fifth century B.C. historian Herodotus, contrary winds had, in fact, driven them off course, and they had ended up on the shores of Egypt. Herodotus described how Paris' mariners had blabbed his wrongdoings to temple priests in Egypt who, in their turn, reported the matter to the king. The king had questioned Paris and was appalled that he had abducted the king of Sparta's wife. He would have killed Paris outright had he not been a visitor of royal blood to his land. Instead, the king decided to keep Helen safely in his care until such time Menelaus came to fetch her. Paris he sent on his way back to Troy.

In the *Iliad* there was no mention of Egypt by Homer, and Helen and Paris were always together in Troy. It is in the *Odyssey* that Menelaus relates his Egyptian adventures to young Telemachus when he comes enquiring after the fate of his father Odysseus. At the banquet celebrating the engagement of his daughter Hermione Menelaus tells the assembly how he and Helen had been stranded in Egypt on their homeward journey as he had failed to appease the gods after the sack of Troy. A sea-nymph had spotted him in Egypt in a state of deep despondency because he had no means of escape. To discover what was preventing his departure from Egypt Menelaus, she said, must somehow catch and pin down her father Proteus (the Old Man of the Sea) who came ashore daily at midday: "*...he lies down to sleep under the arching caves, and around him is a throng of seals, the brood of the lovely child of Ocean; they too have come up through the grey waters, and they too lie down to sleep, smelling rankly of the deep brine below...*" (Odyssey Bk4:401-405) [W.S]

Menelaus must, the sea-nymph went on, have with him three of his most courageous men prepared to ambush and capture Proteus her father. But, she warned him, he would try to foil his captors by "... *taking the shape of every creature that moves on earth, and of water and of portentous fire; but you must hold him unflinchingly and you must press the harder. When at length he puts away all disguise and questions you in the shape he had when you saw him resting, then cease from your constraint; then, O king, let the ancient sage go free and ask him which of the gods is thwarting you and how you are to reach home again over teeming ocean.*"... (Odyssey Bk4:412-419) [W.S.]

By doing all the sea-nymph told him, Menelaus finally managed to sail back to Sparta – accompanied, of course, by his serene but wayward wife, the beautiful Helen.

Helen might be beautiful but she suffered for it; she bitterly regretted that she had broken the social laws of her people, and was often miserably homesick for Sparta and her young child. When Menelaus and Paris faced each other on the plains of Troy to fight their duel, Helen's heart had unexpectedly filled with *...sweet longing for her former husband, and her city and parents...* (Iliad Bk3:139-141)

Helen was the pawn (or the queen) on Aphrodite's chess-board, being moved by her in whichever direction suited her immortal will. I wondered whether the anguish she (Aphrodite) had caused Helen might have been out of jealous spite. As the most beautiful woman in the world, might Aphrodite have felt just a little piqued since she herself was the most beautiful, the 'fairest' of all the goddesses? Some stories claimed Aphrodite to be the daughter of Zeus and Dione, in which case Helen would have been her half-sister.

I pointed to a faint tracing paper outline of an island to the south, and remarked that I thought it must be Kythera, Aphrodite's island.

"Why hers?" Harry asked. He grimaced as he shifted his position on his uncomfortable sharp rock.

"If Aphrodite didn't rise from the sea at Paphos, Cyprus, then it's thought it was there at Kythera, I said."

"Rose from the sea!" Harry snorted.

I didn't tell him the story of how Zeus' father Kronos had cut off the genitals of Ouranos (his father) and was said to have flung them into the sea, and the result had been Aphrodite who rose as the beautiful goddess from the waves. I knew the story would only receive another snort. Instead, I said: "It's been suggested that Paris actually won Helen when she was on Kythera worshipping Aphrodite at her shrine there."

"Which makes a nonsense of the whole Spartan story then." And Harry declared he couldn't sit another second on his rock. When he stood up there were deep indents in the seat of his trousers. We scrambled back up to the pathway and the pine trees. We had accomplished what we'd come for, and Harry said that it was now his turn to choose where to go. He wanted to drive down into the deep Mani region, to see the tower-houses where Maniot families had lived in wild isolation, and where blood-feuds had erupted between families, and vendettas had brought death and mayhem to the area.

We are lost! We are hopelessly lost deep in the Mani, and it is raining heavily! Great cones of mountains seem to stand on sentry duty ahead of us. There is a feeling of wild desolation and I unexpectedly experience intense anxiety. Is it possible that we will never get out of here? The windscreen wipers whip from side to side; the road is awash. Where is the road back to Sparta? Will anybody miss us if we never appear again?

At last through the downpour we see the wet glimmer of headlights approaching slowly through the rain. Harry flashes his lights, and winds down his window, whereupon rain lashes in. The other car stops, and I leap out under an umbrella. Oh, how we depend on human contact. When lost and isolated in such inscrutable terrain, how wonderful the voice of a stranger, even if it speaks Greek, a language I can understand if spoken slowly. "Pou einai tin Sparta?" I ask. "Biddlybiddlybiddly," comes the reply. "Pio siga, parakalo," (more slowly, please). "Milate Anglika?" I am asked. (Do I speak English?) "Nai, nai – yes, yes!" (English, thank God!) "You must go straight – for two kilometres straight, perhaps more – then left." I mime what he is saying, and he nods and smiles at my wet bedraggled state. "Thank you, thank you! Efharisto poli!" I wave my thanks and dive back into the car. Our saviour draws away, and we are on our own again. Harry doubts I have the directions right and quizzes me repeatedly. But I have been fully concentrating, too anxious to make a mistake and remain for ever lost in the Mani. We drive on.

The storm passes and the heavy, massive dark clouds give way to lighter white cumulus. Look, look! A road to our left! And the signpost says Sparta! From great anxiety comes huge relief; after rain comes sun; after darkness, light. I am already thinking of the future. Tomorrow I want to take a trip into the Taygetos mountains. Let's hope we don't get lost up there.

I am often amazed by the fact that humans live their lives planning or imagining a future for themselves; they put into action what they want to do and then live it till it becomes the past – a memory.

The trip into the Taygetos mountains along the Langadha pass was planned with my usual mix of optimism and pessimism – pessimism in the expectation of getting lost, of rock-falls, uprooted trees or crashed cars blocking the road after the storms; optimism in the hope of getting to the other end and back again without mishap. In fact, our only obstacle that day was a flock of multi-coloured long-haired goats idling in the road, a couple lying down and snoozing in the sun, unwilling to move till I waved my arms and shouted 'oy!'

The sun shone, and the tree-filled ravines were sun-drenched, their colours picked out in startling hues of green. The rugged mountain peaks stood out stark against the blue sky. A few white cotton bolls of cloud sailed serenely in the heavens.

As we drove on I spotted a cave about fifty metres up to our right and we stopped in a lay-by to take a closer look. A wooden arrow pointed upwards along a goat track, but prudence took over as progress up the steep track became more hazardous – a broken leg with a car to drive? Thoughts of some calamity occurring and incapacitating us in the future prevented us from risking life and limb in the present.

Instead, we sat on a boulder and enjoyed the scenery – a wooded gorge below the road, and clumps of wild flowers all around us, as well as small saplings and shrubs which had rooted themselves precariously on the steep, rocky slopes. This was the route taken by Telemachus when he came to Sparta from Pylos having enquired of King Nestor if he knew what had become of his father. He and King Nestor's son had taken a day to do the journey to Sparta by chariot.

The Langadha pass brought us out eventually to open countryside with grass and scrub and undulating mountains; it was as though, after suffering a tumultuous convulsion, the landscape had recovered and there were now only minor upheavals. Far below we could see a village, and in the far, far distance was a faint horizontal line which Harry said with confidence was the sea. I liked to think we were looking towards Pylos, the kingdom of King Nestor. It was where I hoped we'd go to on one of our future trips to Greece.

We heard a cuckoo – the first in several years because for some reason the cuckoo no longer makes its annual trip to England.

"Home again tomorrow," Harry said with a satisfied sigh. "Short and sweet, that's what I like."

Our drive back took us past the famous break-away peak of ancient Mystras with its citadel, and from this side we could see several more domed, grey-stone monasteries. We thought that later that afternoon we would pay our respects to it. But, by the time we emerged from a siesta, it was raining heavily again, and we lacked the determination; and so the plan became a memory of what we could have done but didn't.

What is unaccomplished is, of course, of no consequence at all. What is dared and done, and the more foolhardy it is, is what will be remembered. Wasn't Helen a prime example of that? If Homer had not sung his epic poem about the couple and the Trojan War, then we would not know about it these three millennia on.

Helen lived in highs and lows, in light and shade; she knew ecstasy and sorrow. When Aphrodite finished playing with her pawn (or queen) Helen returned to her king and the past became her memory, but one so dramatic that several centuries on Homer entertained an audience with it, and later still it was written down for all the world to read.

As Helen herself said in the *Iliad*: '*...ill-starred couple that we are, that even in days to come we may be a song for the ears of men that will come hereafter.*' (Iliad Bk6:356-358)

# ODYSSEUS

Odysseus was the son of King Laertes of Ithaka and his wife Anticlea. He was married to Penelope, and their son Telemachus was born just before the outbreak of the Trojan War. Odysseus was described by Homer as cunning, resourceful, and a man who spoke with authority. He was quick-thinking, and able to endure great hardship when the odds were stacked against him. In short, he was a James Bond survivor.

Before his marriage to Penelope, however, Odysseus had been a contender for the hand of Helen, and had taken the oath that he would give his assistance to whoever won her if requested. When King Menelaus and Palamedes of Nauflio arrived in Ithaka to recruit him for the Trojan War, Odysseus attempted to break his vow by feigning madness. Yoking an ox and a horse together he started to sow the sandy shore with salt. Palamedes, suspecting this to be a trick, called his bluff by placing the baby Telemachus on the sandy shore before the yoked animals. Odysseus immediately pulled up short, thus showing himself to be perfectly sane and, therefore, honour-bound to keep his oath.

It was after the sacking of Troy and on his homeward journey, described by Homer in his epic poem the *Odyssey*, that Odysseus showed his greatest courage and survival skills. It was to be another ten years before he reached home due to the wrath of Poseidon. During this period his wife Penelope waited patiently, pursued and pestered by many of the local nobles who wanted to marry her. Not knowing the fate of her husband, Penelope used delaying tactics by declaring she had first to finish a shroud she was weaving for her father-in-law Laertes. This she wove by day but secretly unravelled by night. After three years of this ruse a maid betrayed her, and Penelope was forced to complete the task.

By now Telemachus was a young man, and the mantle of responsibility weighed heavily on his shoulders. He was in a quandary about his mother's suitors coming constantly to the palace, and realized it was time to take matters into his own hands. He set out to mainland Greece to enquire of those kings who had returned from the war what they knew regarding the fate of his father.

After many trials and tribulations Odysseus, with the help and guidance of the goddess Athena, was finally reunited with his son, and his wife's patience and faithfulness were at last rewarded.

# CHAPTER 5
# ITHAKA

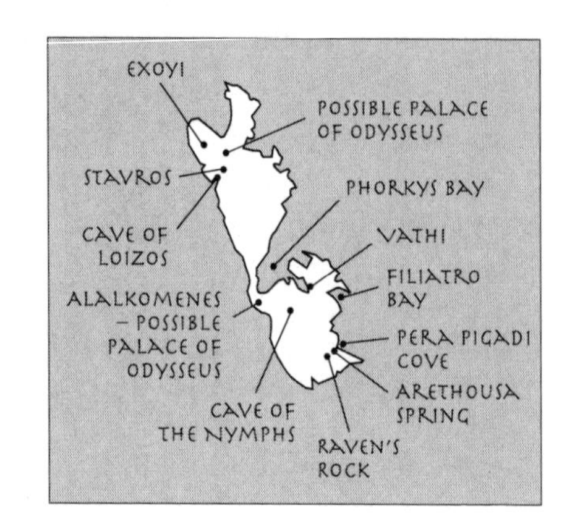


For one who never expects plans to come about without a major disaster throwing everything into disarray, I was pleasantly surprised when we found ourselves approaching Ithaka by sea-taxi from Cephalonia. A gale was blowing and our small boat, appropriately named the *Odysseus*, rose up and smacked down on the waves with extraordinary force which slap, bang, walloped right through me. We'd been advised to sit in the stern as that would be more comfortable. Hell, what was uncomfortable then? I stood up and clung to a hand-rail. The boat continued to smack, bang, wallop along at high speed, but at least I wasn't getting jarred up through my spine to my skull. Harry remained seated with a half smile, half grimace, depending on whether we were riding a wave or crashing down on one. I wondered how the small boat could withstand such buffeting, its structure was taking enormous strain.

A young buccaneer was the proud owner of this boat, and stood at the bows legs astride scanning the horizon. He wore a baseball cap back-to-front, and had on calf-length trousers with multiple pockets. His mate sat at the helm bringing us ever closer to the island of Odysseus.

Our journey by sea would take an hour, unlike Odysseus' which took ten years with one obstruction after another hindering him. To read the *Odyssey* is to be thrown into his adventures. When finally arriving back on his island, Odysseus still had delays and ordeals to overcome before he was reunited with his wife. All these obstacles I hoped to remember while Harry and I visited the places mentioned by Homer.

At last we saw Ithaka, an island with a range of rounded wooded mountains rising from a dark-blue-and-turquoise sea. As we drew nearer we saw that the thick covering of trees ended where slanting strata of creamy-white rock plunged into the sea. It looked beautiful. We passed a number of peaceful sandy coves where the occasional yacht lay at anchor. In time we came to the small whitewashed Chapel of Agios Andreas perched on a rocky outcrop marking the approach to Vathi, the port of Ithaka. Here the sea was calmer and a cobalt blue.

Vathi was a cluster of terra-cotta roofed houses and seaside tavernas around a wide bay. Yachts and small boats were moored up. The *Odysseus* was manoeuvred alongside the quay, and our young buccaneer grabbed a rope, leapt ashore and secured her to a bollard, before helping us out.

What could be easier than to arrive by small boat and to be met by the car-hire firm? We loaded our luggage into a small Fiat and, to avoid any further stress after our long journey, the car-hire firm offered to lead the way to our apartment some four kilometres away.

The balcony to our apartment overlooked mature olive trees which fringed Phorkys bay. It was into this bay that the ship carrying Odysseus had put in after his ten years of adventure following the Trojan War. To take ten years to return home seemed to me excessively inept, but then the gods were against him – well, Poseidon, god of the sea, was

His sea voyage home was fraught with danger, but the most perilous adventures came with and after his visit to the land of the Cyclopes, one-eyed monsters whose occupation was sheep-farming. By some great misfortune one of them was a son of Poseidon by a sea-nymph. His name was Polyphemus, and he captured Odysseus and his crew and imprisoned them in his cave together with his flock of woolly sheep which he always brought in at night. He placed a great rock before the mouth of the cave so there was no escape for any of them. When Polyphemus asked Odysseus his name, he replied cunningly 'Nobody'. That night for his supper to their great horror Polyphemus seized two of Odysseus' companions '*…and dashed their heads against the ground as though no more than puppies. Their brains spurted out over the earth and soaked it. He tore them apart limb by limb for his supper, and devoured them like a mountain lion, till entrails and flesh, marrow-bones and all, were consumed…*' (Odyssey Bk9:289-293)

The next evening Polyphemus again killed and ate two of his men. But by now Odysseus had devised a plan. He gave his captor a bowlful of excellent vintage wine which so pleased him, that he gulped down great quantities of it till he '*...toppled over and fell on to his back on the floor. There he lay with his great neck twisted to one side, overpowered, as all are, by sleep. Wine containing morsels of human flesh was then vomited up from his throat...*' (Odyssey Bk9:371-374)

As soon as this son of Poseidon had passed out, Odysseus sharpened the end of an olive-wood stake and put it in the fire till it glowed red-hot. He and his men then drove it into Polyphemus' one eye, turning it and grinding it in '*...and the blood sizzled round the burning wood. The scorching of the blazing eyeball singed his eyelid and brow, and the roots of his eye crackled in the heat...*' (Odyssey Bk9:388-390)

The Cyclops shrieked, and when his fellow Cyclopes called out, asking who was killing him, he replied 'Nobody', so they ignored him. In the morning Polyphemus fumbled about blindly; he removed the rock from the cave-mouth to let out his sheep, and Odysseus and his men escaped by clinging to the underside of the largest of them.

After surviving that traumatic ordeal, they next arrived at the Aeolian island ruled by Aeolus, lord of the winds. He entertained them well, and they stayed with him for a month. When Odysseus asked about sailing home, his host was very helpful and gave him a leather bag in which he had imprisoned all the winds. Aeolus tied the mouth of the bag with a silver string so not a breath of contrary wind could escape to slow down his journey; only the west wind was allowed to go free to help them sail back to Ithaka. The leather bag was stowed safely away in Odysseus' ship, and for ten days they made good progress. But while Odysseus was asleep his men, thinking that Aeolus had given Odysseus a bag full of gold and silver, were tempted to take a look. As soon as the silver string was untied the wild winds burst out.

In no time they found themselves blown back to the Aeolian island where Aeolus was aggrieved to see them again. He believed that their return showed they had displeased the gods.

And so Odysseus' adventures continued till his final shipwreck when he was washed up on the shores of Phaeacia (thought to be Corfu) where King Alcinous heard his story, and obligingly arranged for a boat to bring him back to this his homeland, to Phorkys bay in Ithaka.

Odysseus had been so weary on arrival that he'd remained asleep while being put ashore by the mariners who'd brought him. A great hoard of treasure was off-loaded with him, gifts from King Alcinous showing the high esteem in which the king held him.

*...There is a harbour of the Old Man of the Sea, Phorkys in the countryside of Ithaka. There two precipitous promontories opposed jut out, to close in the harbour and shelter it from the big waves made by the winds blowing so hard on the outside; inside, the well-benched vessels can lie without being tied up, once they have found their anchorage. At the head of the harbour, there is an olive tree with spreading leaves, and nearby is a cave that is shaded, and pleasant, and sacred to the nymphs who are called the Nymphs of the Wellsprings...* (Odyssey Bk13:96-104) [R.L.]

That evening we walked down to Phorkys bay. A woman lay stretched out on a sun-bed reading a book, otherwise there was nobody about. The shore was fringed with ancient olive trees, and I found one whose gnarled and hollow trunk provided a comfortable seat. I leaned against it and watched Harry make his way into the sea, then plunge forward and strike out till he was about twenty metres from the shore. For a while he swam with his head underwater, and when he came up for air, he shouted 'tur...' and tried to point but went under, re-surfacing to call 'turt...' but disappeared blowing a series of bubbles to the sea's surface.

*...It was into this bay they rowed their ship. They knew of it beforehand. The ship, hard-driven, ran up onto the beach for as much as half her length, such was the force the hands of the oarsmen gave her. They stepped from the strong-benched ship out onto the dry land, and first they lifted and carried Odysseus out of the hollow hull, along with his bed linen and shining coverlet, and set him down on the sand. He was still bound fast in sleep. Then they lifted and carried out the possessions, those which the haughty Phaeacians, urged by great-hearted Athena, had given him, as he set out for home, and laid them next to the trunk of the olive, all in a pile and away from the road, lest some wayfarer might come before Odysseus awoke...* (Odyssey Bk13:113-125) [R.L.]

I settled myself more comfortably into my hollow olive tree, and thought about the goddess Athena and how she'd taken charge of Odysseus and helped with his return and his eventual reunion with his wife Penelope and his twenty-year-old son Telemachus. When Odysseus was put ashore here, Telemachus was absent, having gone off to enquire about his father's fate. Before leaving he'd desperately tried to assert his authority over the numerous suitors who came daily, wining and dining at the palace's expense. He'd taken up the sceptre and stood before them courageously in order to speak his mind but, in his distress and to his dismay, he found himself *in a stormburst of tears.* His attempt at sounding authoritative failed miserably.

But Athena had already put into the mind of this sensitive young man that he should set sail for mainland Greece and enquire of King Nestor of Pylos, and King Menelaus of Sparta what had become of his father. This Telemachus had obediently done which explained his absence when Odysseus returned.

A sleek white yacht sailed silently around the right-hand promontory and dropped anchor in our bay, and several young men dived overboard for an evening swim. With our solitude interrupted, Harry came out of the water and joined me, and soon we were heading up to see the nearby Cave of the Nymphs where tradition has it Odysseus hid his hoard of treasure given him by King Alcinous of Phaeacia.

The sun was low in the west as we drove a few kilometres back to Vathi then took a turning to the right up a steep hill. The sun glowed through the tall dried grasses either side of the road; olive trees and tall cypresses, many of the latter as thin as skewers, cast long shadows in the evening light. It was a rustic scene and we passed plump hens scratching behind a wire-mesh fence, and a few goats nibbling away at the undergrowth. What struck me most was how uninhabited this rural area was; several houses were in a bad state of repair, some without their roofs; but where the houses were habitable there was no one to be seen.

After winding steeply up the hillside for a while, we at last saw a brown notice-board indicating the Cave of the Nymphs. We parked the car under an olive tree, and got out into the cool of the evening. We now had to walk steeply up a paved track. After about fifty metres the ground levelled out, and there in the rocky cliff-face was the triangular mouth of the cave. Unfortunately it was off-limits, and had a padlocked metal gate set in a high wire mesh fence to prevent anybody from gaining entry.

*...a twilit cave, a most lovely one, sacred to those nymphs who are called Naiads; in it are bowls of stone and pitchers of stone; bees also store honey there; and then there are long looms of stone on which the nymphs*

*weave tissues of ocean-purple that ravish the gazing eye. There are streams there too that flow perpetually; and there are two entrances into it, a northern entrance that mortals may descend by and a southern one that belongs to the gods; by this no human being may enter; it is the pathway of the immortals…* (Odyssey Bk13:102-110) [W.S.]

From where we stood at the mouth of the cave we could see Phorkys bay way below in the far distance with its tiny round tree-covered islet at its centre. The northern part of Ithaka loomed beyond to the left of the bay. The sleek white yacht was still there, though there was no sign of anyone either swimming or relaxing on deck.

Harry voiced what I had been thinking: "Why on earth did Odysseus haul all his valuables up to this God-forsaken cave? Surely he could have found somewhere nearer to where he'd come ashore?"

Traditional belief was that it was here at the Cave of the Nymphs, but I had just read that some archaeologists believed Odysseus may have hidden his treasure in a cave in Phorkys bay itself which would make more sense, except its interior presumably wasn't the same as that described by Homer. Unfortunately, the roof at the Phorkys bay cave had fallen in and it was no longer accessible. Other scholars were of the opinion that a cave in Polis bay below the town of Stavros in the northern part of the island, was where the treasure had been hidden, and that Odysseus had come ashore there. Some of the discoveries from that cave were dated to the Mycenaean era; and the artefacts consisted of the sort of gifts King Alcinous would have given Odysseus, such as cauldrons, and bronze tripods. The cave was known as the Cave of Loizos because it was a man named Dimitris Loizos who c.1870 had discovered it. I hoped we would be able to visit it when we explored the northern region of Ithaka.

But first things first.

'*…Your own first task is to journey to the swineherd who has in charge your sows and boars; he is as loyal to you as ever; he loves your son and he loves Penelope. You will find him sitting near the swine as they feed beside the Raven's Rock at the spring of Arethousa, drinking from the deep dark water there and battening upon acorns…*' (Odyssey Bk13:406-411) [W.S.]. These were Athena's instructions to Odysseus on his arrival, and the following day we intended to visit it. The Arethousa Spring was clearly shown on the map.

★

I supposed Athena must have had her reasons for sending Odysseus many kilometres southwards in the wrong direction, and well away from the two possible locations identified by archaeologists as his palace.

We arrived at a signpost indicating the Arethousa spring. A wooden-roofed picnic shelter stood at the side of the road, and along the flank of the treeless hillside, between low scrub-like vegetation, we could see the scored track which disappeared into the distance around a promontory.

The paved pathway looked promising, but the paving ceased after fifty or so metres, and then it was a question of skirting boulders and not tripping over stones. We had our trekking sticks which helped to keep us from falling down the cliff-face. Having rounded the first promontory – and oh, how lovely the shades of turquoise of the sea were, but how hot walking on this treeless track!

We paused for a moment to gaze at the view. "This Arethingummy spring," Harry said, "what's so important about it?" I sensed he was wanting to turn back, but we had plenty of bottled water and I didn't like to be defeated.

"It is important," I said. I hoped I sounded convincing. "It's where the swineherd Eumaus watered his animals."

"I can't imagine anyone in his senses coming along here with a herd of pigs," Harry remarked.

"Talking of pigs, do you remember the story of Odysseus and the enchantress Circe?" I asked.

"I remember the name but not – " He was out of earshot as he picked his way over some slanting-to-the-precipice shale. After I'd joined him on a safer bit of the path, I said: "Circe was the one who turned Odysseus' men into swine and fed them on acorns." And I told Harry how, with the help of Hermes (the messenger god and son of Zeus who'd disguised himself as a young man), Odysseus was rendered immune from Circe's spells by being given a special magic herb. '... *It had a black root, and a milk-white flower. The gods call it moly, and it is an awkward plant to dig up, at any rate for a man, but the gods can do anything...* (Odyssey Bk10:304-306)

Odysseus was ordered by Hermes to draw his sword on Circe, then make her swear an oath to reverse her witchcraft over his comrades, and to assist them on their homeward journey. Hermes warned, however, that if Circe invited Odysseus to her bed, he was to consent. Odysseus obeyed these instructions, and they were treated with such kindness by Circe that a whole year passed. It was his men who eventually had to prise Odysseus away.

We rounded another promontory and saw there was yet another one beyond. I too was tempted to turn back. We were by now like automatons putting one foot forward after another, crooking an arm, unscrewing the cap to the water bottle and taking regular sips. Our bottles were half empty but I supposed we'd be able to refill them at the spring.

On and on and on. Then we spotted a couple picking their way along coming from the opposite direction. When they got near they greeted us. "Is it far?" I asked.

They looked at each other, their shirts clinging to their sweaty bodies. Then the woman retrieved her mobile phone from the back pocket of her shorts.

"It is not near," the man said. "The spring, you cannot go."

"Here you see. You look." and the woman showed us the photos she had taken of the spring beyond a barbed wire fence. The spring itself was the merest trickle of water dampening the moss and ferns which grew around it.

The man pointed to our water bottles and wagged his finger at us, shaking his head. "You cannot," he said.

After their warnings, it seemed to turn back was the only option. We had depended on being able to refill our bottles at the spring. Defeated? Yes. I would just have to be satisfied with the images the woman had shown me: the trickle, the damp moss, the steep rocky hill behind it covered in thorny scrub known as Raven's Rock.

The woman flicked her photos on her mobile screen to show a white pebbly cove with vivid turquoise water down below the spring. "Look – it is Pera Pigadi," she said, and pointed to a cove on the map she had opened up for us.

"Ah." I nodded.

It was there that Telemachus had come ashore after visiting King Nestor and Menelaus. He *...set out on foot and walked at a good pace till he reached the yard where his large drove of pigs were kept and the swineherd slept among them with loyal heart, and none but kindly feelings for his masters' house...* (Odyssey Bk15:555-557)

The woman's mobile showed that three young people were enjoying the solitude of the cove; it was clearly possible to scramble down to it. We, however, would be doing no such thing.

The man, seeing our short supply of water, produced another

bottle from his haversack and gestured insistently that we take it. We thanked him profusely, and the two went on their way, leaving us to follow at our more cautious pace.

The panoramic views of the cliffs and promontories reaching down to the cream-coloured rocks, and the shades-of-turquoise sea never ceased to take my breath away and, in fact, to make the return hike almost enjoyable.

When at last we reached the wooden picnic shelter, we slumped down on the bench, and drained the remains of our water. When we'd cooled down I thumbed through our road map and found another landmark that I wanted to see, the Cave of Eumaus. "It's not much further along this road," I said, indicating the short distance.

"Hum. Well, since we're here, I suppose we have to go," Harry said.

We drove on along the road till we saw the sign indicating Eumaus' Cave to our left. We took a dirt-road to it just wide enough for the car. For several hundred metres we kept going till gradually it narrowed and became quite impassable. Neither of us was going to walk another step in the midday heat.

I would just have to be content to know that somewhere nearby the swineherd Eumaus had had his hut. It was there that Odysseus had spent his first night back on Ithaka; there too that Telemachus had come to meet the swineherd and had found his father whom Athena had disguised as a vagrant.

Because the suitors were out to kill Telemachus, Eumaus was sent back to the palace to inform Penelope of her son's return. While father and son were alone together Odysseus revealed his true identity with the help of Athena who changed him from being an elderly tramp into the great hero that he was. Telemachus to his amazement thought he saw a god before him.

*... 'Why do you take me for an immortal?' said the noble and patient Odysseus. 'Believe me, I am no god. But I am your father, on whose account you have endured so much sorrow and trouble and suffered persecution at men's hands.'*

*With that he kissed his son and let a tear roll down his cheek to the ground though hitherto he had kept himself under strict control...* (Odyssey Bk16:186-192)

Laertes, Odysseus' father, had been in mourning since the death of his wife Anticlea. His only interests now were his orchards and small-holding. I had been reading a book about the island which suggested that, of the two possible locations for the palace of Odysseus, the one in the area known as the School of Homer in the north of the island was considered the most likely. But in the *Odyssey* the swineherd was sent ahead by Telemachus to give news to Penelope that he was back and well; and Eumaus was told not to go on further to inform Laertes. I thought that 'not to go on further' sounded as though the palace of Odysseus must be the one close to Phorkys bay, rather than the one much further north beyond the town of Stavros. Archaeologists are divided on the matter. Well, we would see them both while on Ithaka, starting with the hill of Aetos, the nearer acropolis, the one I thought the likeliest for Odysseus' palace.

Harry and I first drove down to Vathi to look in at the archaeological museum. There we saw many artefacts from the ancient town of Alalkomenes on the hill of Aetos.

The finds on display in the museum were of the right period for Odysseus (c.1250 B.C.) – figurines, pots, coins with the head of Odysseus on one side and Athena on the other, as well as household objects.

Close by the museum we came across a large memorial stone set out on the pavement, and on it I read the name Byron inscribed in Greek. Further down in English I read: 'for the commemoration of Byron's stay at Ithaka August, 1823'. Below that was: 'if this island belonged to me I would bury all my books here and never go away'. I felt surprisingly proud to share Byron's sentiments about the island. Byron left Britain to give what moral and financial support he could to the Greeks at the start of their War of Independence against the Turks. He'd died of a fever at Mesolongi on mainland Greece in April, 1824, the year following his visit to Ithaka. In Greece he is regarded as a national hero, and there is a memorial in his honour in the heart of Athens.

Harry wanted to swim in a cove we'd been told was the most beautiful on the island, so from Vathi we first drove on to Filiatro bay.

Yes, it was beautiful. And it would have been idyllic had not the whole island known it. The parking area was packed with cars, as was the beach with sun-bathers. Smoochy music from the 1950s came from loud-speakers strung up in the olive trees. A taverna served drinks and snacks, and we had freshly squeezed orange-juice seated at one of the tables set out in the shade under the trees. A husky female voice was singing *One enchanted evening...* A few yachts were anchored offshore, and the sea was its own indescribable shades of turquoise.

When Odysseus was washed up on an island called Oxygia, he was held captive for seven years under the spell of another enchantress called Calypso. She '*...was singing in a beautiful voice as she wove at the loom and moved her golden shuttle to and fro. The cave was sheltered by a verdant copse of alders, aspens, and fragrant cypresses, which was the roosting-place of feathered creatures, horned owls and falcons and garrulous choughs, birds of the coast, whose daily business takes them down to the sea. Trailing round the very mouth of the cavern a garden vine ran riot, with great bunches of ripe grapes; while from four separate but neighbouring springs four crystal rivulets were trained to run this way and that; and in soft meadows on either side the iris and the parsley flourished. It was indeed a spot where even an immortal visitor must pause to gaze in wonder and delight...* (Odyssey Bk5:61-69)

The husky female voice crooned on: *...You may see a stranger/ You may see a stranger/Across a crowded room...*

For 'room' read 'cave'. Odysseus was completely bewitched by Calypso, and might have stayed indefinitely if, after seven years, Athena hadn't intervened. The goddess went to her father Zeus, and pleaded with him to help free Odysseus from Calypso's clutches. Zeus sent Hermes, the messenger god who'd saved Odysseus from his year with Circe, and he reasoned with Calypso till she reluctantly agreed to help Odysseus build a raft on which to sail away. Unfortunately, Poseidon was still angry with Odysseus and, seeing him on his way home on a raft, sent down a violent storm. *...a monstrous wave crashed over him from above, driving upon him violently and whirling his raft round and round. He was thrown out clear, having let the steering-oar slip from his hands. A hideous tempest of wrestling winds descended on him, snapping his mast in two while sail and sailyard were tossed to a distance in the sea...As a violent wind tosses a heap of dry chaff and scatters it all this way and that, so the wave now scattered the raft's long planks. But Odysseus bestrode a single plank, like a man riding a horse...* (Odyssey Bk5:312-317,368-371)

Here at Filiatro bay, it was difficult to imagine any storm. The sea was a stretch of sparkling calm, and sleek white yachts sailing silently – *...so fly to her side/and make her your own/or all through your life...*

Harry went in for a swim, while I amused myself watching a wealthy looking middle-aged father trying to keep a semblance of authority over his three teenage sons. He was reclining on a sunbed with a book perched on his stomach. His sons were attempting to impress their teenage girlfriends and were determined to show they were independent of parental control. Their mother was a well preserved beauty, oblivious to the goings-on around her. She was a sleeping enchantress – a Calypso dreaming of her Odysseus.

The strange hypnotic charm of Filiatro bay (never mind the crowds), and the down-memory-lane smoochy music, made it hard to leave. But depart we had to, and we left to a voice singing ... *Going on a sentimental journey/Sentimental journey home...*

We are on the hill of Aetos, my favoured location for the palace of Odysseus. Aetos is Greek for 'eagle' which is strangely apt for this narrow neck of land with its two wide wings representing the north and south areas of the island. It is an isolated spot with nearby dilapidated shacks and signs of a possible gypsy encampment.

On the lower slope is the Chapel of Agios Georgios, a relatively modern building, re-built several times due to earthquakes. I am interested that it is dedicated to St. George because I've read that here on the acropolis summit are the ruins of a temple or sanctuary thought to be of Apollo. Christianity liked to stake a claim on former pagan sites. If there was once a temple of Apollo here, then a chapel dedicated to St. George would be appropriate because St. George killed a dragon, and Apollo killed a Python/dragon, both symbols of evil. Delphi, Apollo's famous oracle site, has such a church built in the fifth century.

When Odysseus eventually arrived at his palace, disguised by Athena as a ne'er do well old vagrant, but one who had news of Odysseus, it had been the feast-day of Apollo. Although disguised, Odysseus announced that on his travels he'd learned that Odysseus was alive and, furthermore, he would appear ... *'Between the waning of the old moon, and the waxing of the new, he will come back to his home and will punish all that offer outrage there to his consort and his noble son.'...* (Odyssey Bk14:162-164)

In those days the first day in the lunar calendar was sacred to Apollo. Apollo arrived at Delphi with a drawn bow, and it surely has some significance that this played a part in Odysseus' return when the suitors were challenged to string his bow and show their skill in archery.

On the other hand, I am aware that Odysseus was under Athena's protection, and that Apollo during the Trojan War was on the side of the Trojans. Maybe I am just trying to read what I want into things. But it is because of his temple here on the hill of Aetos, and of Apollo's lunar festival, that I believe Odysseus' palace was on this acropolis, and not in the northern wingspan of Ithaka.

Harry is roaming around outside the chapel, and finds it unlocked and so we enter; its interior is sparsely furnished with just a few icons, so there is nothing to detain us. Outside a large bell hangs from the branch of an olive tree and inevitably Harry gives it a clang; it has a surprisingly resonant tone which remains vibrating in the air for some while.

It is an ideal location for a palace, because from the path along which we walk we can see the sea both to the west and the east; the island of Cephalonia looms to our west, and to the east the southern part of mainland Greece.

The track we are walking along comes to a dead-end, and we can find no way here to go on up to the acropolis. So we turn around and climb up its side on rough terrain between stunted holm-oak and olive trees. We soon come across a Cylopean wall with Cyclopean steps ascending to several terraces. We climb the steps with care because some of them are only wide enough for a toe-hold.

So here inside the walls is where they think Odysseus' city and his palace might have been. The views are fantastic but I still cannot understand the goddess Athena's motives. Why, if Odysseus was put ashore at Phorkys bay, roughly four kilometres away, did she first send him off to see Eumaus, the swineherd,twenty or so kilometres to the south? Why put him to all that bother, and why also disguise him as a vagabond when he came to his palace to meet the suitors and his wife? Why not let him come as himself? Show himself as the returned husband to the suitors, of which there were over a hundred, and give them a piece of his mind?

Harry cannot help me, but says there must be a good reason for it. You can't have a story if you start at the end. You have to have a series of crises or nobody will listen. People like drama, and the Greeks more than anybody. Suspense, he says, lies in keeping people suspended – well, waiting and alert.

I remember how finally the swineherd Eumaus arrived at the palace with Odysseus. (Eumaus still had no idea he was his returned master). ...*Meanwhile Odysseus and his trusty swineherd had arrived;*

*but they paused for a moment outside when the notes from a well-made lyre came to their ears...Odysseus took the swineherd's arm, and said to him: 'Eumaus, this must surely be Odysseus' palace: it would be easy to pick it out at a glance from any number of houses...the courtyard wall with its battlements is a fine piece of work and those folding doors are true defences...I gather too that a large company is there for dinner: one can smell the roast, and someone is playing the lyre. Music and banquets always go well together.'* (Odyssey Bk17:260-271)

If this is where the palace of Odysseus was, then it would be somewhere here that Odysseus' old hunting dog called Argus would have been lying on a dung-heap. He had been left to fend for himself which I thought disgraceful negligence on the part of the palace staff, and even of Penelope who surely couldn't have been unaware that Odysseus' favourite pet was not being properly looked after.

"If I was waiting for you while you were away," I say to Harry, "I wouldn't spend my days wailing about it, I'd make sure your favourite dog was fit and well and ready to greet you on your return. Penelope may have been a faithful wife, but what a bore she was. She was either in floods of tears or weaving a shroud for her father-in-law. Why be put upon by all those suitors when she only had to say she didn't want to marry any of them, and remove all food and drink. She'd have done better to have fed the dog."

*...Stretched on the ground close to where they stood talking, there lay a dog, who now pricked up his ears and raised his head. Argus was his name. Odysseus himself had owned and trained him...But now, in his owner's absence, he lay abandoned on the heaps of dung from the mules and cattle... There, full of vermin, lay Argus...But directly he became aware of Odysseus' presence, he wagged his tail and dropped his ears, though he lacked the strength now to come any nearer to his master. Yet Odysseus saw him out of the corner of his eye, and brushed a tear away...* (Odyssey Bk17:300-305)

Odysseus then drew his swineherd's attention to the dog who, in recognition of his master even though disguised, gave a feeble wag of its tail, and promptly died. Eumaus described the animal's strength and vigour when Odysseus first had him: '*...you'd be astonished at his speed and power. No wild animal that he gave chase to could escape him in the forest glades. For beside all else he was a marvel at picking up the scent...*' (Odyssey Bk17:315-317)

Heinrich Schliemann, the self-made German millionaire, had been guided by the *Odyssey* as to the whereabouts of the palace and was confident it was here. Cicero, who lived 106-65 B.C., also believed that the hill of Aetos was the location for the palace. Yet later scholars thought otherwise. What had been their reasons?

Well, the following day we planned to go north beyond Stavros to look for the other palace of Odysseus in the area that is known as the School of Homer.

★

There was something about the colour of the sky which suggested it might rain, so we threw our anoraks into the back of the car. We drove north to Stavros, taking the road along the east side of the island, intending to return by the road on the west.

At one point we stopped at a lay-by because from there was an almost aerial view back along the coastline to the port of Vathi. We could make out Phorkys bay as well as the bays beyond Vathi, possibly Filiatro, and further still the promontories along which we'd walked hoping to reach the Arethousa spring. Dark clouds were massing on the horizon and looked ominous, and it wasn't long before the sun disappeared behind them. Soon the clouds were overhead and the first splashes of rain fell. Then suddenly there was a downpour and a flash of lightning followed by thunder. When the storm passed, another could be seen over mainland Greece where a grey curtain of rain was descending at a slant from leaden clouds. Dramatic flashes of forked lightning zipped down from the sky's darkness to the sea.

It reminded me of Odysseus' adventures as he recounted them at the court of King Alcinous: '*...Zeus thundered and struck the vessel by lightning. The whole ship reeled to the blow of his bolt and was filled with sulphur. My men were flung overboard and tossed round the black hull like sea-gulls on the waves. There was no home-coming for them: the god saw to that...*' (Odyssey Bk12:415-419)

But there had been other more treacherous moments at sea in Odysseus' homeward journey. The Siren Voices, for instance. They were bird-like women who sang so beautifully that mariners who heard them were hypnotically drawn towards them and their certain death. Knowing of their danger Odysseus told his men to plug their ears with beeswax, and instructed them to lash him to the mast and to tighten his bonds if he began to struggle to get free. In this manner they managed to get safely past.

There was also a perilous narrow passage which had to be navigated between Charybdis (a deadly whirlpool) and Scylla (a sea monster with six heads, each head with a mouth containing triple rows of teeth). As Odysseus recounted to King Alcinous:

*'...fiendish Charybdis sucked the salt water in. When she spewed it forth, she seethed and swirled throughout all her depths like a cauldron set on a great fire, and overhead the spray fell down on the tops of the two rocks. But when she sucked the sea-water in, one might look right down through the swirling eddy while the rock roared hideously around her and the sea-floor came to view, dark and sandy. Ashy terror seized on the crew. We had looked her way with the fear of death upon us; and at that moment Scylla snatched up from inside my ship the six of my crew who were strongest of arm and sturdiest. When I turned back my gaze to the ship in search of my companions, I saw only their feet and hands as they were lifted up; they were calling to me in their heart's anguish, crying out my name for the last time. As when a fisherman on a promontory takes a long rod to snare little fishes with his bait and casts his ox-hair line down into the sea below, then seizes the creatures one by one and throws them ashore still writhing; so Scylla swung my writhing companions up to the rocks, and there at the entrance began devouring them as they shrieked and held out their hands to me in their extreme of agony...'* (Odyssey Bk12:234-253) [W.S.]

I had read that the early Christian Fathers had used the stories from the *Odyssey* to illustrate the Christian's need to steer a course of right living between the forces of evil, i.e. between Charybdis and Scylla. As for the Siren Voices, they represented the seductive lure of women which at all costs was to be resisted. Re-vamping the Homeric stories had been a good way to draw pagan minds to the new Christian religion.

We came to a signpost and took the left-hand turn to Stavros. I secretly wanted to see the Cave of Loizos but so far had said nothing, knowing Harry would be none too keen. Caves for him were too often way off the beaten track, their mouths securely barred and locked, or just plain disappointing.

We are seated at a taverna in Stavros which is perched on top of a cliff so we have views looking out over the wooded promontories either side of Polis bay. Yes, we have just visited the Cave of Loizos which, as Harry predicted, was yet another non-event. We'd followed a narrow footpath flanked by undergrowth, and the cave itself, when we'd eventually found it, was off-limits with an unimpressive entrance amongst large boulders.

Despite Harry's scornful comments regarding it, I was glad we'd made the effort. I'd read that traces of temple worship had been found there, together with a votive offering with the name Odysseus inscribed on it. There is evidence that Odysseus had been worshipped there as a cult-hero.

Seated at our taverna Harry now spots what he claims is an eagle, and then another soaring above the wooded promontory to our right. I think the birds look more like buzzards, but prefer the idea of eagles so accept his identification. I am reminded of the eagles which Zeus sent as an omen to the young Telemachus in the *Odyssey* when he saw two eagles attack each other predicting the doom of the suitors at the palace. ... *These for a while sailed down the wind...wing to wing. But as soon as they were directly over...where the sound of voices filled the air, they then...fell to work with their talons, ripping each other's cheeks and neck on either side, and so swooped eastward over the house-tops of the busy town...* (Odyssey Bk2:148-154).

"Do you think Homer really was blind?" I say. "If he was, then how on earth could he have described so many things with such vividness and accuracy?"

"Like his storms and shipwrecks?" Harry suggests.

"Or his account of the interior of Calypso's cave," I say.

Certainly Homer's descriptive powers suggest he'd once had remarkable vision and a retentive memory, or else his imagination was fed by details given to him by others.

From our taverna we walk across to the small municipal park close by with tall pines and eucalyptus trees, wooden seats, and a large bust of Odysseus on a tall plinth. A notice-board shows a reconstruction of Odysseus' palace as it might have looked with various rooms identified from details given in the *Odyssey*: courtyards, the banqueting hall, underground store-rooms, and Penelope's private quarters where she would have sat weaving her shroud.

After scrutinizing it for a while, we make our way back to the car and head off to see what the latest archaeologists claim to be the real palace of Odysseus.

★

Not many kilometres north of Stavros we saw a sign to the left pointing down a track to 'Homer's School'. A man we had spoken to in

Vathi had told us he'd been to what he believed to be the Mycenaean palace ruins in the north, and advised us to park our car by the roadside and continue on foot, and he'd given us careful directions. Others we'd asked, had merely shrugged and said the ruins were impossible to find.*

Either side of the path was wooded, and every so often the whiff of sun-drenched rosemary wafted to us on the air. We saw busy bumblebees and butterflies amongst the sun-dried grasses and tangled undergrowth of wild flowers; and through the skewer-thin cypresses, olive trees and pines, we caught occasional glimpses of the turquoise sea.

In time we came to an ancient looking stepped pathway to our left signposted to Exoyi. This was the path we had been told to take. Harry led the way up the steps, and we immediately came to another wooden picnic shelter with a table and benches and a wooden roof similar to the one at the start of the track to the Arethousa spring. We were glad to sit in the shade for a while to cool down. I thumbed idly through my *Odyssey* and came across a list I'd made of Homer's often repeated sayings: *the circling of the years*, or *dawn showed again with her rosy fingers*. Also the adjectives he used for people, such as: *much enduring Odysseus, resourceful Odysseus, circumspect Penelope, thoughtful Telemachus,* and so on.

I read them out to Harry, and then said: "This morning I was reading how in those days a man of noble birth was expected to earn what was known as *kleios*, meaning the good opinion of other people. Not only that but to gain *kleios* for himself meant he was also adding to the esteem of his father. Family honour was all important. The heroic age of Odysseus was a matter of earning and keeping *kleios*, a good reputation." I turned to Harry, and said: "Don't you think that's rather nice?"

"Is that why Penelope's suitors were so frowned on?" Harry queried. "Because they turned their backs on your klissy thing, and preyed on the palace day after day?"

"I suppose so."

We gathered our water bottles and went on up the stepped pathway. We'd been told that after about a hundred metres we should strike off to the right through the trees, and we'd come across the ruins. After several false attempts we spotted two roofless stone buildings, one of which had a Cyclopean wall built with enormous blocks of dark grey boulders.

From there the view was superb to the east, to a bay which, after

* The large Cyclopean ruins that we found I suspect were not the excavated site, though in the right location.

the storm of the morning, was whitish shades of blue merging to intense turquoise. I was to learn later it was Afales bay. Beyond, on the horizon, loomed mainland Greece.

I perched myself on a Cyclopean boulder. I thought how it seemed excessive for Odysseus to kill all those one hundred plus suitors, and said as much to Harry.

Harry was seated on the ground chewing on a stalk of dried grass and following his own line of thought. He removed it, and said: "A vagabond? Very odd! I wonder why his goddess wanted to disguise him as a tramp?"

"Maybe Athena wanted to see if the suitors would redeem themselves by welcoming a homeless beggar and offering him food and hospitality – one of the first rules in those days was hospitality and generosity to a stranger at your door." Then I added: "Instead, one of the suitors threw an ox-hoof at Odysseus which showed what louts they were. They scoffed at him for daring to approach the palace. In fact, Odysseus earned more *kleios* then by showing great forbearance at their taunts."

After the ox-hoof incident, Telemachus spoke up furiously and reprimanded them but, flushed with wine, the unruly suitors only laughed uproarously: *...with jaws that were no longer their own... their eyes were bursting full of tears, and their laughter sounded like lamentation...* (Odyssey Bk20:347-349) [R.L.]

One of the palace seers named Theoklymenos spoke out, foreseeing future doom for them.... *'Unhappy men,' he cried, 'what blight is this that has descended on you? Your heads, your faces, and your knees are veiled in night. There is a sound of mourning in the air; I see cheeks wet with tears. And look, the panels and the walls are splashed with blood. The porch is filled with ghosts. So is the court – ghosts hurryng down to darkness and to hell. The sun is blotted out from heaven and a malignant mist has crept upon the world...'* (Odyssey Bk20:351-357)

After the suitors' unseemly behaviour, Athena took matters in hand and inspired Penelope to announce she would marry whoever was able to string the ancient bow belonging to Odysseus; she was well aware that only he had formerly been able to do it. The bow was thought to have once belonged to Heracles and had been given as a gift to Odysseus.

By degrees Odysseus' true identity became apparent. Eurycleia, his faithful nurse, was the first to see through his disguise by recognizing a scar on his leg when she bathed his feet, the result of being gored by a wild boar when a young man; and now by being the only one able to string the bow and skilfully fire arrows through the holes in twelve axe-heads.

*...resourceful Odysseus, once he had taken up the great bow and looked it all over, as when a man, who well understands the lyre and singing, easily, holding it on either side, pulls the strongly twisted cord of sheep's gut, so as to slip it over a new peg, so, without any strain, Odysseus strung the great bow. Then plucking it in his right hand he tested the bowstring, and it gave him back an excellent sound like the voice of a swallow.*

*Taking the string and the head grooves he drew to the middle grip, and from the very chair where he sat, bending the bow before him, let the arrow fly, nor missed any axes from the first handle on, but the bronze-weighted arrow passed through all...* (Odyssey Bk21:404-411,419-423) [R.L.]

Odysseus had already seen to it that all other available weapons had been hidden away, and the women were barricaded safely in another part of the palace.

*...Shedding his rags, the indomitable Odysseus leapt onto the great threshold holding his bow and the quiver filled with arrows...*(Odyssey Bk22:1-3) Taking revenge at last on one of the leading suitors named Antinous, he stopped him as he was on the point of drinking wine from a two-handled goblet of gold. *...No thought of bloodshed had entered his head. For who could guess, there in that festive company, that one man, however powerful he might be, would bring calamity and death to him against such odds? Yet Odysseus shot his bolt and struck him in the throat. The point passed clean through the soft flesh of his neck. Dropping the cup as he was hit, he lurched over to one side. His life-blood gushed from his nostrils in a turbid jet. His foot lashed out and kicked the table from him, the food was scattered on the ground, and his bread and meat were smeared with gore.*

*When the suitors saw the man collapse, there was an angry outcry in the hall. They sprang from their chairs and rushed distraught about the room, searching the solid walls on every side. But not a shield or sturdy spear did they see to lay their hands on...* (Odyssey Bk22:11-25)

With proof now of his identity, and having given the signal to Telemachus, he and the loyal palace staff began the slaughter of all the suitors.

*...They lay in heaps in the blood and dust, like fish that the fishermen have dragged out of the grey surf in the meshes of their net onto...the beach, to lie in masses on the sand gasping for the salt sea water till the bright sun ends their lives...* (Odyssey Bk22:383-388)

Odysseus, and those faithful to him, then had the unpleasant task of removing the bodies, and purifying the palace before Penelope could be allowed back down to welcome the return of her husband.

As though reading my thoughts, Harry suddenly said: "Over a hundred bodies! It must have been quite shocking for Penelope to come to terms with the ruthlessness of her warrior husband."

"And dispiriting for Odysseus when, despite all the proofs of his identity, Penelope remained aloof and distant," I said. "On the other hand, I suppose, if you had left me for twenty years, and had then returned and murdered my admirers, I might have considerable misgivings about you. Anyway, I'd want to know why, if it really was you, you'd stayed away so long. In fact, I might wonder why you'd bothered to come home at all since you'd obviously had other more interesting things to occupy your time."

Harry was supposed to say that had it been him, of course he'd have come back immediately. Instead, he said something akin to not blaming Odysseus staying under the spell of Calypso for *as many circling of the years as possible* since she sounded quite charming with her cavern, trailing plants, her owls and sweet singing and her weaving. After seven *circling of the years* (he particularly liked that quote) it was surprising he'd ever left her. He put the dried stalk back into his mouth and chewed it pensively.

"He and Calypso actually had a son," I said. "It was the gods who, possibly taking pity on Penelope, decided Odysseus should return."

"Not that Homer made his home-coming an easy happy event," Harry mumbled with his stalk of grass between his teeth.

"No, it was traumatic. Penelope was quite unwelcoming and suspicious."

Harry removed the stalk. "I'm surprised he didn't sail back to his dear Calypso. I would have done."

I let it pass, then said: "After twenty years the poor woman needed to adjust to the sudden changes in her circumstances – the death of all her suitors, and this vagrant displaying the strength and accuracy in archery of Odysseus. She needed more proof poor thing. At least Odysseus had the wit to realize he needed to woo his wife all over again."

"Um."

Odysseus ordered the palace staff to wash and dress in their finest clothes, and called for music and dancing.

*...The men washed and donned their tunics, while the women decked*

*themselves out. The admirable bard took up his hollow lyre and had them soon intent on nothing but the melodies of song and the niceties of the dance. They made the great hall echo round them to the feet of dancing men and women richly clad…* (Odyssey Bk23:142-147)

More importantly, Odysseus saw to his own ablutions before attempting any amorous advances on his wife.

*…Athena also played her part by enhancing his comeliness from head to foot. She made him look taller and sturdier than ever; she caused the bushy locks to hang from his head thick as the petals of the hyacinth in bloom…* (Odyssey Bk23:151-154)

But, although Odysseus looked *…like one of the everlasting gods…* his wife still remained distant and, in exasperation, Odysseus ordered a bed to be made up for him to sleep alone. At this Penelope tested him with something only Odysseus would know could not be done; in this she was as cunning as Odysseus. She ordered Eurycleia, Odysseus' nurse, to remove their marital bed and place it outside. This she knew was an impossibility because Odysseus had fashioned it himself from a living olive tree around which he had built their bedroom. Only Odysseus himself would know this. He responded by describing in detail the work he'd had in constructing it. With this proof of his identity Penelope's *…knees began to tremble as she realized the complete fidelity of his description. All at once her heart melted. Bursting into tears she ran up to Odysseus, threw her arms round his neck and kissed his head…* (Odyssey Bk23:206-209)

"Everyone in floods of tears including Odysseus," Harry said with a touch of scorn. "But there you are, that's the Greek way, I suppose."

A large butterfly came fluttering by and landed on a myrtle bush. It was possibly four inches in diameter when its wings were outstretched: a creamy white with black lines up its wings, a giant-like version of the cabbage white. For a while we followed the butterfly's movements till it floated away. Our minds came back to where we were, the great Cyclopean dark grey walls, the greens of the trees, and the distant vivid turquoise of the sea edged with white where it was breaking against the cream-coloured rocky cliff-face.

While we sat the sun shone warmly, though we were cooled by a light breeze. And all the while the cicadas sang like Siren Voices casting their spell over us. Eventually, however, Harry planted his trekking stick into the ground, rose to his feet and declared it was time to move on. "Let's go and see Exoyi," he suggested. "I'm not walking there, but we can drive."

Well, why not? We had completed what I had come for.

★

So here we are at Exoyi where we have an unimpeded aerial view down to Afales bay. This is the oldest village of Ithaka and is built amphitheatrically around a natural hillside. So this is where the stepped pathway would have brought us had we followed it.

A strange thing happens to me while here. I have spotted the blue dome of its church perched high up the village and, as though drawn by an invisible hand, I leave Harry beside the car without saying anything to him and begin to walk up through the village until I come to steps which lead to the church. The invisible hand draws me on to the church courtyard where I find a couple of women seated on benches outside the entrance gossiping together. They tell me the church is locked and that it is dedicated to Agia Marina. It isn't until later that I find out that it is believed there was once an ancient temple up here. Could it have been a temple of Athena who played so great a part in Odysseus' life? Her temples were, as far as I knew, always on high elevations.

I find it incredibly difficult to get away from this church, and keep finding myself back there. How to find the road again to get back down to the car? The two gossiping women say it's impossible to get lost in Exoyi. But I can. When I leave the church, whichever alleyway I take somehow brings me back to the church in an uncanny manner. I begin to worry that Harry will be tearing his hair out wondering where I've got to.

In fact, when I eventually get back to this one and only should-have-been-easy-to-find road up which I'd come, I find Harry in the car waiting.

I tell him about the 'pull' of the church, and he dismisses it as a non-event.

"Like a divine power drawing me there," I say.

Harry waves a foreign currency jacket thing at me and asks why it is being used as a book-mark in my copy of the *Odyssey*. Do I know it contains several hundred euros? He's been wondering where all our money had gone.

"A divine power has led you to it," I remark.

"Nothing divine about it, I happened on it purely by chance!" Harry scoffs.

"So we can eat out tonight instead of cooking?" I ask hopefully.

Harry's silence is a good sign, and I take the money and put it in my bag.

★

After we return from our evening meal in Vathi, we sit out on our balcony with mugs of coffee. From the balcony next door we hear the murmur of voices speaking English.

The couple we see there must have just arrived so have the pleasure of some days ahead of them on Ithaka. We sadly can only look back on the days now past. The sky is a darkening violet with a half moon in the sky together with the glittering evening star. The sleek white yacht has sailed away, and the small tree-covered islet is a dark grey silhouette. The olive trees fringing the shoreline are a shadowy silvery-grey, the sea is oily black in the tranquil bay.

I read the first lines of the *Odyssey* to myself:

*Goddess of song, teach me the story of a hero.*

*This was the man of wide-ranging spirit who had sacked the sacred town of Troy and who wandered afterwards long and far. Many were those whose cities he viewed and whose minds he came to know, many the troubles that vexed his heart as he sailed the seas, labouring to save himself and to bring his comrades home...* (Odyssey Bk1:1-6) [W.S.]

And so our final evening ends.

We are back in our sea-taxi, and the buccaneer stands again feet astride at the bows with, on this occasion, his father at the helm. What could be easier than parking our hired car at the quayside and leaving the car-keys under the mat as instructed by the car-hire firm?

I brace myself for the smack, bang, wallop journey back to Cephalonia but, on the contrary, there is no gale this morning. It is comparatively calm as we depart from the world of imagination and extraordinary adventures, to the reality of our modern world.

We pass landmarks we recognize: Filiatro bay, then the track we took to the Arethousa spring and the white pebbly cove of Pera Pigadi below it, then Stavros and the Cave of Loizos.

Gradually our small boat leaves the coastline of Ithaka which grows smaller as we head for Cephalonia from where we will fly home. *Nostos*! The word is Greek for home-coming and the English word 'nostalgia' comes from it – I feel nostalgia for the island we have left behind, and say a silent goodbye; by now it is a mere shadow on the horizon.

# KING NESTOR OF PYLOS

Nestor was the son of King Neleus of Pylos. After an attack on the kingdom, when his father and all his brothers were killed, Nestor inherited the throne. At the time there were many raids between neighbouring monarchies when valuable livestock was seized. Whenever Nestor suffered such losses he responded in kind. For example, when King Augeus of Elis stole a team of his horses intended for the chariot race at the Olympic Games, Nestor retaliated by seizing a large number of Augeus' cattle, including a hundred and fifty horses, as well as fifty chariots.

He was brought up to be a strong athlete and became a skilled sportsman, winning many prizes. It is, however, the Trojan War for which he is best remembered. He was believed to have been sixty when the war began and, therefore, seventy at its conclusion. During the course of the war he drew on his years of experience, and was never reticent in offering his opinion. His advice was always politely listened to, if not always taken.

Two of Nestor's seven sons accompanied him to the Trojan War: Antilochus who was killed in action, and Thrasymedes who returned safely home to Pylos with his father.

# CHAPTER 6

# PYLOS

Our trip to Pylos began with a bang – literally. I was gazing at the bay of Navarino, with its long island of Sfacteria stretched across its two promontories, and didn't notice a step as I came down from our hotel. Harry, seeing me tumble, shot out an arm to catch me but succeeded only in turning me over so that I crashed down backwards on the concrete path. Rising slowly from my somewhat undignified fall with my skirt around my ears, I found I was still able to move, and only had a rapidly swelling lump on the back of my head. Despite it, I felt surprisingly fit and unshaken. Twinges of pain at the base of my spine were a slight anxiety, though I said nothing and found that I could walk quite easily and, with care I could sit down without discomfort.

Harry's concern and constant questioning merely reminded me that I wasn't feeling dizzy, wasn't nauseous, hadn't broken my neck or impacted my vertebrae. For a while we sat on the hotel terrace with the view to the sea. Modern Pylos was an attractive small port whose cream-coloured square houses with their terra-cotta tiled roofs clustered around the bay.

That first evening found us at a taverna looking out over the tranquil bay. Soft Greek bazooki music played in the background. The sun was setting, and for a moment glinted through a great gap which pierced a distant rocky islet. Between the long thin island of Sfacteria and one of the mainland promontories, a solitary pinnacle of rock like a dog-tooth rose from the sea.

Navarino bay was all but landlocked, and had been the site of a decisive naval battle in the Greek War of Independence. A monument to the three British admirals who'd helped overthrow the Turks in this victorious battle stood in the arcaded square in the centre of Pylos.

Later that evening we took a leisurely walk along the promenade. Small tavernas were lit up and doing brisk business. The cool of the evening was bringing the community out for their evening stroll after the heat of the day.

A long jetty stretched out from the promenade where a few boats were moored. We strolled along it to the far end where a large coast-guard vessel, bristling with sea-going equipment, was moored; beside it was a large, gleaming white gin-palace of a private yacht.

What a contrast to the ancient wooden vessels with their oars and sails which had once put to sea taking King Nestor's army off to the Trojan War. Nestor had sailed with ninety ships from the old port of Pylos.

Having proved to Harry (and myself) that I could walk and sit and climb steps, I felt confident that my plan to visit King Nestor's palace the next day could go ahead. I gave silent thanks to the powers-that-be that I was still mobile, and not laid up in a hospital bed.

"Always look down when you're walking," were Harry's last words to me that night as he switched off the light.

King Nestor was the eldest of all the Greek warriors. He was a just man, and greatly respected; he was also kindly, generous-minded and wise.

It has been suggested that Nestor's character reflected the landscape which nurtured him. Certainly, as we drove the sixteen or so kilometres north towards his palace, the scenery was of gently undulating olive groves, distant mountains, and the occasional assertive conical hill which thrust itself upwards commanding attention. Such hills were said by many to have sacred qualities.

We arrived at Nestor's palace, and walked up the long approach to its entrance. The whole archaeological area was protected by an impressive cream-coloured roof-covering, with a surrounding walkway from which visitors could look down on the excavations.

"King Nestor?" Harry queried, "What's special about him?"

"Well, he was the eldest of the Greek warriors?" I said, posing it as a question.

"How old?"

"Sixty," I replied. Then I added: "Sixty at the start of the war, which means he was seventy by the time the war ended."

"Still fighting at seventy? Good God!"

Due to the respect in which he was held because of his age (implying wisdom), Nestor was listened to when giving advice – something he did at every opportunity – though his advice was seldom taken. Achilles and Agamemnon were given an earful regarding what Nestor saw as serious shortcomings in their characters in their stubborness over the beautiful slave-girl Briseis:

'*...This is, indeed enough to make Greece weep!...Now listen to me. You are both my juniors. And what is more, I have mixed in the past with even better men than you and never failed to carry weight with them, the finest men I have ever seen or shall see...*

'*Agamemnon, forget the privilege of your rank, and do not steal the girl. The army gave her to him: let him keep his prize. And you, my lord Achilles, give up your rancour against the king. Through the authority he derives from Zeus, a king who holds the sceptre has more claim to our respect. You, with a goddess for mother, may be the stronger of the two; yet Agamemnon is the better man, since he rules more people. Agamemnon, be appeased. I, Nestor, beg you to relent towards Achilles, our mighty bulwark in the stress of battle.*' (Iliad Bk1:255-263, 276-284)

And despite Nestor's three score years and ten – and how often did he complain about not being the man he was and the feebleness that comes with old age – he was, in fact, surprisingly strong. In the middle of a battle his trace horse (a third horse which ran alongside the two pulling the chariot) was hit by an arrow: *...In its agony it reared up, for the point sank into its brain; and writhing round with the arrow in it, he threw the other horses into confusion.*

*Nestor rushed in with his sword and was slashing at this horse's reins when Hector's horses came galloping up through the turmoil, with...Hector himself...And the old man would then and there have lost his life but for the quick eye of Diomedes...who saw the danger and gave Odysseus a...call for help...* (Iliad Bk8:85-93)

Yet Nestor then mounted Diomedes' chariot and went straight back into the thick of the fighting. Nestor was one of the few Greek warriors to return home safely, and it was amazing to think that this was where the old warrior had lived in his palace.

We began the tour of the ruins. Despite the notice-boards giving detailed explanations, or maybe because of them, I soon became totally confused by the ruined walls of hallways, lobbies, pantries, corridors and so on; I found it difficult to get excited about water-cisterns and drain-pipes. Only when we came to the enormous *megaron* (the Throne Room) with its great round hearth at its centre did I become alert and focused. Its grandeur was striking and, even though the floor was of hard-packed earth, it was easy to imagine how it must once have looked. At one time there had been great fluted wooden columns standing on round stone bases, the latter still in place. Also the throne itself, though not quite centrally placed, had stood against the far wall where its stone base was still to be seen.

From the numerous finds it was believed that the floor had been of paving slabs in a variety of geometric patterns, and the ceiling had been richly decorated in a similar fashion. The walls had been plastered and painted with colourful frescoes depicting such things as hunting and battle scenes; frescoes of lions and griffins had decorated the wall behind the throne.

During his long reign King Nestor had acquired great wealth; the customary cattle-rustling of his day, no doubt, had helped fill the palace coffers. While in Troy he'd recalled at length the part he'd played in it as a youth: '*... What a haul of booty we rounded up from the plain – fifty herds of cattle, and as many flocks of sheep, as many droves of pigs and scattered herds of goats, as well as a hundred and fifty chestnut horses, all of them mares and many with foals beside them. In the night we drove them in to Neleus' city of Pylos, and Neleus* (Nestor's father) *was delighted that a novice warrior like myself should have had such luck...*' (Iliad Bk11:679-684)

To Harry whose livelihood had been farming, this was a decided black mark against King Nestor. All that pious sacrificing of bulls and sheep when they were stolen, he objected – all that banqueting and feasting on other people's animals – what crooks! And as for the gods themselves, what sort of gods could they be accepting all that so-called stolen sacrifice without complaint! And Harry thanked God for the ten commandments and particularly the one that said 'Thou shalt not covet thy neighbour's ox.'

Having made his point on the Almighty being a superior moral God than all the scallywag Olympians, we turned to look at the view to the south of the palace. From there olive groves stretched away to a strip of sea in the far distance – would that have been where Telemachus had sailed in to enquire of Nestor if he knew what had happened to his father Odysseus? Or had the sea in those far distant days come further inland closer to this palace?

When Telemachus came, he'd been accompanied by the goddess

Athena disguised as Mentor (a friend of his father). Telemachus had never been away from home before, and the presence of Mentor/ Athena must have been reassuring to the inexperienced young man. It couldn't have been easy for him to sail to mainland Greece with the sole purpose of seeking an audience with King Nestor.

They happened to arrive on a feast-day of Poseidon when black bulls (stolen?) were being sacrificed to the god. King Nestor was seated on the seashore with his sons. When they saw Telemachus and Mentor/Athena arrive, Peisistratus, Nestor's youngest son, went forward and took the hand of each in turn: *...he seated them on soft fleeces above the sea sand, by his father himself and his brother Thrasymedes. He gave them portions of the inwards and poured them wine in a golden cup, then spoke in greeting to Athena, daughter of Zeus who holds the aegis: 'Friend, offer prayer to Lord Poseidon, for it is his feast you have chanced upon at your coming here. And when you have prayed and poured libation in ritual fashion, then give your comrade the cup of honey-sweet wine to pour with; doubtless he too is a worshipper of the Deathless Ones, because all men stand in need of the gods. But he is a younger man – indeed of my own age – so it shall be to you first that I offer this cup of gold.'...* (Odyssey Bk3:37-48) [W.S.]

Athena approved of young Peisistratus, and rejoiced to find him so right in thought and deed. She prayed earnestly to Poseidon to grant Telemachus success in his mission and a safe return to Ithaka. *...Thus she prayed and all the while was herself bringing the prayer to its fulfilment...* (Odyssey Bk3:60-61) [W.S.]

After they had eaten. Nestor asked his guests why they were there, and was told by Telemachus that he was seeking news of his father Odysseus. This set Nestor off on a long reminiscence about the horrors of the war, and those who had lost their lives, such as Achilles, Patroclus, and his own son Antilochus. He then praised the brave Odysseus: *'...none was bold enough to challenge Odysseus in strategy; in cunning of every fashion he was supreme – your own royal father, if indeed you are his son; as I look at you I am filled with wonder. All you say has a perfect rightness; who would have thought a man so young could display such rightness in his speech?...'* (Odyssey Bk3:120-125) [W.S.] And he went rambling on. Finally he admitted that to tell the whole story of the horrors of the war might take five or six years and everybody's patience would wear thin and they would head for home. Yet he still continued, recounting the tragic homecoming of Agamemnon and then the troubles Menelaus experienced. Eventually *...the sun* *sank and darkness came...* Athena tactfully intervened and suggested they pour a libation to Poseidon and the gods, and then retire to bed. She declined Nestor's invitation to sleep in comfort at his palace, with the excuse that she had pressing matters to attend to and must return to the ship to give orders to the crew early the next morning. Before the goddess abandoned her charge, however, she asked Nestor to provide Telemachus with horses and a chariot to take him the next day to Sparta to find out from Menelaus if he knew what had become of his father. And she also asked that one of his sons accompany him. *...So spoke the goddess of gleaming eyes, then went from them in the likeness of an osprey. Amazement came upon all who watched it, and aged Nestor was astounded to see such a thing with his own eyes. He took Telemachus by the hand and said: 'Dear child, I think you will prove no coward and no weakling; you are still a boy, yet even now you have gods to go with you and protect you...this is none but the daughter of Zeus,...she who always favoured your noble father among the Argives...'* (Odyssey Bk3:371-379) [W.S.]

With Athena gone, Nestor prayed, and promised Athena he'd sacrifice a heifer in her honour. Then Nestor *...led the way,...walking to his own splendid halls before his sons... When they reached the king's noble palace, they began to take their places on higher and lower seats; when they were all there, the king himself mixed into the bowl a delicious wine, eleven years old, which only now the housekeeper had unstopped and opened. Such was the wine that Nestor drew on, and as he poured a libation from it he uttered earnest prayer to Athena, daughter of Zeus...* (Odyssey Bk3:384-393) [W.S.]

After all had drunk, they retired to rest in their own homes. Nestor, however, kept Telemachus back; he was *...to sleep in the palace precincts, in an inlaid bed under the echoing portico; and beside him he put Peisistratus, already a spearsman and commander,though the only son still at home unmarried. The king himself slept in an inner room of the lofty palace, and the queen his wife shared his bed...* (Odyssey Bk3:397-401) [W.S.]

"So the old boy had a queen?" Harry asked. And I told him about Nestor's wife Anaxibia who'd remained a good and faithful wife and, therefore, totally unheard of, unlike Helen and Clytemnestra.

"I'm all for adultery," I said. Harry gave me a penetrating look. "I mean it's adultery that makes a literary masterpiece, not faithfulness."

"Ah!"

We continued around the walkway and reached the Northeast

Gateway and Court. It could have been there that Telemachus had slept *under the echoing portico*, near the Queen's Hall.

Close to the Queen's Hall was a bathroom. Along the far wall was a bath (not a full-length one as might be expected today) but a hip-bath set in its original stucco-coated clay base. Around the inside rim was a design of whorls.

It could well have been there that, when dawn came, Telemachus was *...bathed by Nestor's youngest daughter; this was the lovely Polycaste* (whom he later married)*; she bathed him, anointed him well with oil, then dressed him in handsome cloak and tunic. He came from the bath looking like a god...* (Odyssey Bk3:465-467) [W.S.]

True to his word, Nestor that morning sacrificed a yearling heifer, then ordered his sons to yoke up the horses to a chariot for Telemachus. Nestor's young son Peisistratus went with him, and they set off at speed for Sparta.

By now we too were ready to leave, though not at speed but with some reluctance. I took one last look at the strip of sea in the distance. Over there on a headland was what was known as the cave of Nestor. Apparently, the gun-ho Heinrich Schliemann, who'd excavated Troy and Mycenae, had visited the cave and, in his customary scratchings around, had discovered Mycenaean pottery. It had been these finds, together with several royal beehive tombs in the vicinity, that convinced scholars there had to be a royal palace nearby. And so excavations had begun, and this great palace complex had been unearthed.

The first dig had commenced here on the hill of Englianos in April, 1939. With the first trial trench they'd found almost immediately exciting things such as portions of painted and plastered walls, broken pots and, most rewarding of all, a number of inscribed clay tablets in a hitherto unknown script. Everything was of the Mycenaean period, and the conclusion drawn was that the site was one of the greatest importance – Nestor's palace, no less. World War II had put a temporary stop to the work, and it wasn't till 1952 that digging was resumed and the whole palace complex had come to light.

The clay tablets were to become known as the Linear B tablets, and there were over a thousland of them. Thanks to the dedication of the young British scholar, Michael Ventris, the tablets with their hitherto unknown ancient script and hieroglyphs were eventually deciphered and found to be an inventory of the goods and chattels held by the palace. They listed the amount of olive-oil, wine, grain, the number of chariots, chariot-wheels, gold, jewellery, textiles and so on.

The archaeologists of the day were ecstatic. The names of several cities were also deciphered with gifts offered from far and wide to the king which suggested he was highly regarded and influential.

We left the great archaeological site and drove on four kilometres to Chora where there was a museum which exhibited the finds from the palace. There we saw a number of highly decorated *pithoi* (large ceramic jars for oil or grain), their shattered pieces painstakingly reassembled. The same love and care had gone in to the piecing together of two-handled *amphorae* used for transporting and storing goods, mostly wine. We saw bronze daggers with rusty blades, great portions of frescoed walls, gold artefacts, jewellery – but only one Linear B tablet, and that a replica, the originals being in the National Archaeological Museum in Athens.

Harry declared it was time to return to Pylos, time for food, time for a siesta –

"Mind that step!" he reminded me for the 'nth time as we came down from the museum. And for the 'nth time I dutifully obeyed, giving thanks to the gods also for the 'nth time for delivering me from disaster the day before. Tomorrow was set aside for Nestor's cave, and I needed to be in peak condition to get to it. So far, so good.

We've made extensive enquiries how best to get to Nestor's cave, and have been told which route to take for the shortest and easiest ascent. Following directions, we find ourselves bumping along a bamboo and reed-flanked dirt-road heading for Voidokoilia bay where we park beside a lagoon. Here there are no buildings of any sort to spoil the landscape, and we begin our long walk over the soft pale sand around the bay of Voidokoilia – Homer was right in singing about 'sandy Pylos'.

Is it here, perhaps, that Telemachus dropped anchor on his arrival? Here that he and Mentor found King Nestor and his men sacrificing black bulls to Poseidon on the god's feast-day?

The sea is a mix of turquoise and aquamarine. We've been advised to wear shoes not sandals as it is easier to trudge through soft sand in shoes, and later over hard rocks when climbing to the cave.

Harry stops and, raising his stick, he points halfway up the side of the tree-covered distant promontory. "There!" he says. I follow the line of his stick and see the mouth of the cave, and my spirits soar with excitement and anticipation. There is no time to waste, however, because it is already getting hot – the time is nine-thirty.

Trudging through soft sand is hard-going. Nevertheless, after fifteen or so minutes we reach the sand-dunes below the cave. As we wade through the sand up the dunes, we pause briefly in the shade of a stunted pine as a young man comes bounding down the track.

"Have you come from the cave?" I ask.

The young man stops and says cheerfully, "Yes, I have." He speaks impeccable English which isn't surprising as we find he is English.

"Is it difficult to get to?"

"Not really. It's just – well, a bit demanding, but well worth a visit! I'm afraid I'm in a tearing hurry. My family's waiting and we're flying back today." He waves a hand, and goes bounding on down.

Harry murmurs something about that fellow being much younger than us and we can't expect to do what he can do. But, like King Nestor, age to me just means doing what you can and coping with difficulties as you confront them.

"We can always turn back," I say with confidence. I start up the narrow track and Harry feels he must stay with me. Stunted trees offer spasmodic shade, otherwise there is only low scrub and bushes. It is hot but there are shady spots where we can stop to drink from our water bottles.

Slow but sure – choose carefully where to place your feet – make certain your stick is planted firmly in a groove in a rock, or on the ground to give you leverage for the next foothold higher. It is a slow business but, nevertheless, we go progressively up.

And we arrive! Yes, we've achieved our goal!

I look out from the great mouth of the cave to the fantastic view below of turquoise sea and golden sand; to the sand dunes, and the distant reeds and rushes around the blue lagoon; to the mountains beyond. Unless I'm badly mistaken, we are surely looking in the direction of Nestor's palace – and there too beyond is a conical hill.

The cave is also known as Hermes' cave. In Homer's *Hymn to Hermes* the god was born to the nymph Maia who was secretly loved by Zeus who visited her after dark while Hera slept. In due course Maia gave birth to Hermes at dawn, and by midday he'd already set out to explore the world and had killed a tortoise and with its shell had made the first lyre ever. He then stole Apollo's cattle, but was cunning enough to drive them backwards to the cave so it would look as though they were leaving it, and he fixed brushwood to his own feet to disguise his tracks.

Popular belief is that here was where he hid them. At any rate, Apollo came *...to goodly Pylos, seeking the shambling kine...* Hermes, however, was a cunning infant and, as Homer put it, quickly climbed back into his cradle and *...sank down within his fragrant swaddling bands...and curled himself, feet, head, and hands, into small space... his tortoise-shell he kept beneath his armpit...*

When Apollo accused the baby of stealing his cattle, Hermes denied it, and was quite prepared to swear an oath on his father's head – *So spake he with twinkling eyes, and twisted brows, glancing hither and thither, with long-drawn whistling breath...*

Apollo was not taken in by such a display of innocence, and dragged Hermes to Mt. Olympus to be judged by Zeus. His father saw through such trickery and falsehoods, and ordered him to return the cattle immediately. To cut a long story short Apollo, despite his anger, found himself amused by the sheer audacity of this precocious half-brother of his, and the two eventually were reconciled.

In later life Hermes became a messenger of Zeus. It was he who helped King Priam take the wagon-load of treasure to Achilles' hut to ransom back Hector's body. It was Hermes also whose task it had been to accompany the souls of the dead to Hades. In the *Odyssey* he'd marshalled the souls of the slaughtered suitors of Penelope with his golden rod *...he roused them...and they followed him, thinly gibbering. As in a recess of some eerie cave a chain of bats may be hanging downwards from the rock, but one of them drops from the clinging cluster and then all the rest flit squeaking round, so did these ghosts travel on together squeaking, while easeful Hermes led them down through the ways...to the fields of asphodel, where the...phantoms of the dead, have their habitation...* (Odyssey Bk24:4-13) [W.S.]

We enter the cave. It takes a while for our eyes to adjust to the darkness. Gradually we see it is only an outer cave, a sort of ante-room with a Gothic-like arched entrance leading through to another.

We enter the second cave and find ourselves in an immense, cathedral-like cavern with a fissure high above through which a little light shines. The colours of the interior are incredible; there are hues of blue-grey, russet-purple, pinky-blue, whitish-bluey-pink, yellowy-creamy-white, and the deepest bottle-green. The light penetrates from the first cave entrance more than from the fissure above and we notice several deep clefts around the rockface, but they lead nowhere. In one area the structure of the rock resembles the scraggy udders of old cows;

the beginnings of stalactites, only an inch long, look remarkably like teats; water dripping from them could be mistaken for milk – milk to feed the baby Hermes? Or milk from Nestor's cattle that were said to be brought into this cave?

We both stand in awe; there is such profound silence here; such a feeling both of peace and sanctity. To one side there is a depression about two metres in diameter where the earth looks as if fires were once lit and sacrifices and burnt offerings were made to the gods.

We wander around this huge spell-binding cavern. If Nestor was a cattle-rustler, a great number could be concealed here, though getting them here might be difficult.

We turn to leave and walk towards the light flooding in through the mouth of the cave. The light dazzles us as we step out from the darkness, and it takes time for our eyes to adjust again; we pause to look at the sandy bay, the lagoon and the distant mountains, before we begin our slow and cautious descent.

Once safely back down to the sand-dunes we are elated by our success; the cave surpassed our expectations, and we surpassed the expectations we had of ourselves. We meet a couple who are clearly considering whether or not to do the climb. The man is good-looking with piercing green eyes. He is a Clint Eastwood super-star, and points upwards with a questioning look. "You come down?" he asks, noting our shouldn't-be-able-to-do-it-at-your-age maturity. Harry feels he's killed a dragon and basks in his new heroic role. "Just take it slowly," he advises. "Nothing to it – and well worth the effort!"

Clint Eastwood makes a sweeping bow, and says (we think he's Italian): "Complimenti!" His beautiful companion smiles, and we watch as they begin their upward climb on their strong brown legs.

The trudge back along the pale, sandy shore of the bay is a slog but there is a spring of success in our step. By now the sun is high in the heavens, though a cooling offshore breeze helps a little.

Driving back along the dirt-track Harry unexpectedly pulls in beside a shack of a place which offers cold drinks. It is set in an olive grove but is hardly the place I've imagined to celebrate our climb to the cave. Large upended cable-reels serve as tables; much of the seating consists of hammered together planks of wood, though there are a few old basket chairs which we seize. In an attempt to provide shade, three sails have been stretched out horizontally over the seating area.

It is private enterprise on a lower scale of things. The owner is making a living of a sort and, despite these makeshift furnishings, we are given delicious, freshly squeezed orange-juice. Harry worries about germs but has only himself to blame for stopping. He is slightly cheered when two cyclists arrive and dismount. They are red-faced and perspiring. The man is about fifty, tall, and has a certain grace and dignity about him as he removes his helmet and hangs it from his handle-bars. His puce-in-the-face wife (who could be beautiful but is, oh, so unlovely after her strenuous cycling), also removes her helmet revealing long blonde hair tied back in a pony-tail. They both have an air of prosperity, and I wonder why they are cycling at all. How glum they are! All their energy is spent. They lick icecreams silently as they try to recharge their batteries.

After a while we break through their listless misery, and learn that they are German. They have come to this shack to get water. Yet they refuse to buy the large bottles which are all that are available. No, they say, they must cycle on to the next stop to buy smaller bottles. Oh, the weariness of cycling in the heat!

I am astonished when quite soon I see the man stand up, an authoritative arm towards his wife who rises with a blank expression, and they put on their helmets again. She mutters to me in an aside that her husband is a restless spirit, must always be on the move, and we watch as they mount their bikes, press glumly down on the pedals, and are once more on their way.

We get thankfully into our car and head back to Pylos, passing – oh, the pity of it! – the cyclists. It would be unkind to wave.

Back at the hotel I pick up a book I have bought on the history and mythology of Pylos, and begin to read about Paleokastro, a thirteenth century Frankish castle on the Koryphasion acropolis. It crowns a great headland to the north of Pylos, and Nestor's cave is on its eastern slope. The hill of Englianos with Nestor's palace is further north still.

In the book the two words 'ancient Pylos' have grabbed my attention, together with the name of the second century A.D. travel-writer Pausanias. I rummage around and find a list of notes I've brought with me, and find a passage I photocopied from Pausanias before we came out. Pausanias had journeyed through mainland Greece giving an eye-witness account of all he saw. Interestingly, I find that the Koryphasion acropolis was one of the places he'd visited. He described in some detail the ancient town of Pylos, built by a man of that name, who'd then been overthrown by Nestor's father Neleus. Pausanias wrote: *Neleus as king made Pylos so important that even Homer in his epic calls it city of Neleus. There is a sanctuary of Athena there with the title Koryphasian Athena, and what they call Nestor's House, which has a painting of Nestor in it. Nestor's monument is inside the city, the one a little distance from Pylos is said to belong to Thrasymedes* (Nestor's son). *There is also a cave inside the city, where they say Nestor and even before him Neleus used to herd their cattle…* (Pausanias BkIV:36)

So where did that leave THE Nestor's palace we'd seen? Could it in fact have been the house of Thrasymedes? Or was Pausanias mistaken? The questions niggle quietly.

I tell Harry I have to see this thirteenth century Frankish castle.

"Oh? Why?" He knows full well there must be an underlying reason other than the castle.

When I tell him about ancient Pylos and Pausanias, and the discoveries of Mycenaean pottery there, Harry says "Ah!". He takes out his map. "Where is it, then?" He's been hoping for an idle day but knows any quest regarding Nestor comes first.

After much mulling over our road map, and enquiries at the hotel reception yet again, we are told with great patience exactly what route to follow to get to the track which will lead us up to this castle.

We are again on a dirt-road fringed with bamboos and reeds, similar to the one we took to Nestor's cave. We park the car at the foot of the acropolis with a lagoon on one side, and Navarino bay on the other – so many different lagoons and bays, I am quite fuddled by them all.

We begin the steep ascent, and soon see a track to the right signposted to Nestor's cave. Before, we'd been advised to take the other route to it as it was shorter.

We are not long into this arduous ascent to Paleokastro when we have to step aside to allow a young couple with a baby in a sling, to pass us. The infant is sound asleep on his father's chest. He is certainly no Hermes full of newborn energy and able to kill a tortoise and make a lyre. He's just a heavy lump which his father has to carry on this long, demanding climb to the castle.

Like Nestor, I would at that moment like to give these parents my advice but, unlike Nestor, with age I have learned discretion and so stay silent. I would like to ask them bluntly why they haven't put a sun-bonnet on their infant's head. But I only say stupidly, 'Oooh, you have a baby!' In fact, in the course of that morning, I see several hatless young children under the blazing sun being dragged around, and I never say a word about what I see as gross parental negligence.

On our slow ascent we pause frequently and admire the occasional pink cyclamen growing from crevices in the rock, or from the parched ground. We enjoy seeing miniature lizards which dart away as we disturb them. After a long upward slog we finally arrive at the great entranceway to this abandoned Frankish castle. We read a sign warning visitors to be wary of old water-reservoirs lying concealed beneath dried grass and brambles. After centuries of occupation – first the Franks, then the Venetians followed by the Turks – the castle has been left to the mercy of the elements, and most of it has slowly but surely fallen down.

Here and there within the castle's extensive ramparts are a few remaining crumbling walls. The ramparts and watch-towers themselves are in a bad way; but the views all around from this acropolis are superb: westwards to the open Ionian sea, to Sfacteria and the straits to the south, north to Voidokoilia bay, and east towards the lagoon beyond Nestor's cave.

"I can't think why the archaeologists don't suppose Nestor's palace is up here," I say to Harry, as we sit on the bottom step to the ramparts to cool down after our climb. "The one they say is Nestor's palace has no defence walls, whereas up here is just about impregnable with its bird's-eye views all around. No approaching enemy would stand a chance."

"Well, don't ask me," Harry says dismissively. "The archaeologists must know."

I mull the matter over. The craze for digging up the past didn't start till the nineteenth and twentieth centuries and then the castle was occupied. Nobody in their right mind would destroy a great castle to see what lay beneath it centuries earlier.

Having got up here, Harry has an urge to walk the ramparts. I myself haven't the nerve. I can see great sections of it have fallen away to the sea, with sheer drops to the rocks below. "Is that wise?" I ask. But he ignores me. Having no head for heights, I am content to have reached the castle itself. Harry has no fear and, handing me his bottle, climbs the steps to those ramparts. The castle covers a vast area, and I can see two distant small figures walking along a section of them on the eastern side.

I continue to read my guide-book about the castle. Suddenly I come to an explanation regarding why Pausanias thought the palace was here. Apparently, in the years following Alexander the Great, the inhabitants of old Pylos spoke about this as being the site and so they had erected a building to commemorate the fact, naming it Nestor's Palace. In his day there would have been no trace of the one we'd seen on the hill of Englianos as it had been destroyed by invaders.

And yet – and yet – I read on. In 1958 (six years after they'd unearthed the palace which exists today), a certain Professor Marinatos believed Pausanias and the earlier Pylians had been right; he'd been convinced they would never have erected their commemorative palace but for the long-held beliefs of the inhabitants. Marinatos, therefore, began his own excavations on the northern slopes here and, while Mycenaean pottery had been found, it had otherwise only revealed Hellenistic houses and early Christian graves.

Oh, Marinatos, why didn't you dig deeper? Did you run out of money? Did you feel defeated by the 1952 excavations going on at the hill of Englianos pronouncing their success? These questions continue to niggle.

If this is indeed the site of Nestor's palace, then it would have been down in the bay below that Telemachus had come ashore. I see from my booklet that near where we have left our car was once the old port of Pylos. Surely to God, it all adds up? It would have been down there that King Nestor and his subjects sacrificed their black bulls to Poseidon.

I look around the extensive area within the castle walls, and wonder where Pausanias' sanctuary of Koryphasian Athena would have been – Koryphasian Athena (so-called after the acropolis itself). But I suppose it and all other buildings disappeared long ago.

Ten minutes pass before Harry comes back from his exploration, exhilerated by the views from atop those ramparts. He is very happy, and declares that he'd like to live here. And if Nestor was wise – as everybody said he was – then he certainly would have built his palace here, and not where it is said to be. So what happened to poor old Nestor in the end, he asks? I tell him that nothing is known about his death, but die he did at a ripe old age.

When we finally get down again, we take a look at the sea where large grey-black blocks of stone are half-submerged in the blue translucent waters. Are these the remains of the old port? We paddle in order to cool down. I am now well satisfied that we have completed my search for King Nestor's palace. "Now," I say to Harry, "you can swim, and we can both relax."

We return to Pylos, and walk into the town square to find a taverna. A jolly-faced fellow catches our attention and beckons us: 'Elate, elate!' His face is so welcoming that we follow him, and he entices us in to see what his wife is cooking in the kitchen. She is a contented looking middle-aged woman with iron-grey hair tied back from her care-worn pleasant face. She draws from her many ovens great oval metal dishes one after the other for our inspection: one contains chicken pieces in a sauce, another sautéed potatoes, another a pork casserole, yet another roasted courgettes, aubergines and peppers, and another beans cooked with herbs in olive oil. I try a little Greek which pleases her and ask for a plate and a serving spoon. I take a spoonful from several of these tempting dishes, and the woman beams with pleasure. Harry is also handed a plate so he can fill it with what he fancies.

When we are seated outside at a table on the pavement, a young man asks us what we'd like to drink. He is their son, and tells us that because it is his mother's name-day (her name is Sophia) the drinks are on the house as a gift. We are surrounded by happy faces, and assure the jolly-faced proprietor that we will return that same evening.

It is getting dark when we return. Sophia is now seated outside surrounded by well-wishers. Her grey hair is no longer tied back and she has taken trouble with her appearance as she waits for friends and family to come and greet her on this her name-day. I give her a small gift and she kisses me on both cheeks. "She's not cooking?" I ask, and am told that two of her sons are at work in the kitchen tonight. Can we go and help ourselves as we did earlier, I enquire?

We are accompanied to the kitchen where the two young men look a little flustered. We help ourselves and are very happy with what we have chosen.

We tell Sophia and her friends that we went up to Paleokastro this morning. This brings expressions of disbelief, then a chorus of 'Bravo!'

I try not to swell with pride, and do not add that we did Nestor's cave the day before. I'm wary that excessive pride might bring down on me a sharp rebuke from on high – another fall, this time with a cracked skull or a broken leg.

At the end of the meal we are presented with a small glass each of Masticha, a special liqueur gathered from the mastic tree, the best growing only on Chios, Homer's island. I feel like Nestor who, at the funeral games of Patroclus, for which he was too old to compete was, nevertheless, given an award just for being there. Achilles told him: '*...The prize I am giving you has nothing to do with the sports; for I know that you will not be boxing or wrestling, nor entering for the foot-race or the javelin...*' To which Nestor replied: '*...Yes, my dear boy,...My feet are not so steady now,...and my arms no longer swing out as they used to once when boxing...*' (Iliad Bk23:620-622, 627-628) He might claim to be feeble, but absolutely not when he cut free that trace horse when it was wild with pain having been wounded by an arrow. It is amazing what an older person can do when he/she has to – or in my case wants to.

I take a sip from my small glass. It is surprisingly potent with a fresh flavour all its own. Harry and I raise our glasses to each other. Then I turn to the seated Sophia, hold up my glass to her and, with the customary Greek name-day greeting, I say: "Kronia polla!" ('may you have many years!'), and she beams with pleasure and inclines her grey head in acknowledgement.

# ACHILLES

Achilles was the son of King Peleus of Phthia, a kingdom in northern Greece, in the Mt. Pelion region of southern Thessaly. His father was a hero in his own right having sailed with Jason and his Argonauts. Achilles' mother was the goddess Thetis, daughter of Nereus (a sea-deity) whose home was a grotto deep down in the Aegean sea. The Judgement of Paris was the direct consequence of their wedding because Eris (Discord/Strife), who had not been invited, came anyway and, in a fit of pique, threw down a golden apple with the words on it 'for the fairest'.

When Achilles was born of this union, his mother tried to immortalize him. Some say this was done by dipping him in the river Styx. To do this she had held him by the heel, and so it remained for ever mortal and, therefore, vulnerable, hence the 'Achilles' heel' saying. Others, though, believe that Thetis attempted to make him immortal by anointing him with ambrosia by day and at night placing him in the embers of a fire to burn away his mortality. When she was caught doing this by her husband he was horrified and, because Thetis was extremely upset that Peleus did not trust her divine powers, she left both him and her son, and returned to her cavern under the sea.

As a consequence, Achilles was placed in the care of Cheiron, a centaur who was half-man, half-horse, and lived in a cave on Mt. Pelion. Cheiron was kindly and wise, and learned in medicine and music. He taught the young Achilles to run faster than any man alive. He also taught him the art of warfare.

CHAPTER

# 7

# MT. PELION

It was mid-September and our third day in the Mt. Pelion region. We were seated on the terrace of our guest-house having breakfast – yoghurt and honey with several annoying wasps circling around. The guest-house stood high above the town of Agios Ioannis in the north-east of Pelion – one hundred and nine steps to be exact, to climb every evening after eating at a taverna by the sea.

The journey here from the port of Volos in the south was indelibly stamped on my mind. We had taken the road which wound endlessly up the densely forested mountain slopes. From the village of Ano Volos, a few kilometres above Volos, we'd stopped to take in the aerial view of the port. At that moment it had been a vast spread of sun-illuminated white buildings huddled together in the plain far below with its shipping, yachts and ferry-boats, and its crab-claw peninsulas holding the Pegasitikos gulf in its grip; the evening light had been throwing shadows on the low mountains either side, and the sea had been a quicksilver grey caused by the rays of the setting sun.

A sculpture of a centaur at Ano Volos reminded us we were in centaur territory – centaurs were the mythical beasts of antiquity, half-man, half-horse. It was on Mt. Pelion that the noble and just centaur Cheiron had lived in a cave and it was he who had been entrusted with the upbringing of the young Achilles. Before Achilles, Cheiron had had the care and education of young Jason – Jason who'd set out with the Argonauts to bring back the Golden Fleece; also of the god Asclepius' two sons Machaon and Podalirius who'd acquired their medical skills from Cheiron and then, as young men, had sailed with Achilles to Troy where they'd tended the wounded.

When driving over the Pelion mountains I hadn't expected such dense forests, or such a rich variety of deciduous trees: beech, oak, maple, plane, but especially sweet chestnut. The latter were at their most majestic, laden with plump spiky husks bursting with chestnuts dangling from the branches like large multiple green baubles. We'd passed the occasional solitary truck and seen families harvesting the chestnuts, packing them into sacks. Several kilometres from our destination here at Agios Ioannis we'd also passed line upon line of wooden, brightly coloured beehives. Cheiron, the centaur, was said to have been the first to teach the art of bee-keeping to the people of the area.

We had come to Pelion for Achilles, but I was discovering that the grown man, the warrior Achilles who'd been larger than life when we'd been in Troy, was strangely elusive here on his home territory. It was his parents, King Peleus and his mother Thetis, who took centre-stage, and also Achilles' mentor Cheiron whose presence seemed to pervade the area.

Although Achilles was one of the most memorable of all the Greek heroes, his fame was not so much due to his outstanding strength and courage as to his passionate beliefs and emotions which caused him to commit the one unforgivable sin of any warrior, that of laying down his arms and positively refusing to fight. All his distress and emotional turmoil regarding King Agamemnon's arrogance in demanding his beautiful slave-girl Briseis are written about in the chapter here on Troy.

Once Achilles had decided on his line of action – or rather, inaction – no amount of bribes and peace-offerings from Agamemnon to get him back on to the battlefield could move him. Not even when Odysseus came and attempted to persuade him with the promise of the return of his beautiful Briseis would he change his mind. Odysseus did his best: ... *'My old friend, when your father Peleus sent you from Phthia to join Agamemnon, he gave you this advice: "My son, Athena and Hera, if it is their will, will give you the strength. You must keep a grip on that proud spirit of yours. Camaraderie is best. Avoid destructive quarrels, and Greeks of all ages will look up to you unfailingly."*

*'That was your father's advice – which you do not remember. But even so, yield, now. Give up this heart-rending fury. Agamemnon would like to make you ample compensation as soon as you relent. Listen while I enumerate the gifts he promises...'* And Odysseus listed tripods, gold, cauldrons, racehorses, women, and so it went on. But, above all, there was the promised return of Briseis: ... *'He will give you all these things,*

*and also the woman he took from you, the daughter of Briseus. And he will give you his solemn oath that he has never been to her bed and slept with her...as is usual...'* (Iliad Bk9:253-263, 272-278)

When his childhood friend Patroclus, despairing of Achilles' intransigence, took up arms and, wearing Achilles' armour, led the Myrmidons to battle and consequently was killed, only then did the shock of it move Achilles to go raging back on to the battlefield. His desolation and anger at the death of his beloved friend were all-consuming. The pain of it caused him to fight with all the strength, courage and heroism that had been instilled in him as a child by Cheiron, whose dwelling here on Pelion was a cave.

"So what about this wretched cave of yours?" Harry demanded, pouring more honey on to his yoghurt with one hand and waving away a wasp with the other.

"Cheiron's cave?" I felt the cave needed to be given due honour and raised up from Harry's level of being a 'wretched' cave since it was where Achilles had spent his early childhood. That morning I had spoken to Nikos who was part-owner of our guest-house and who spoke good English. When I'd asked him the whereabouts of Cheiron's cave he'd looked blank. Yet Dimitri, a personable young man who worked in the local Tourist Information Office in Agios Ioannis, claimed to know its whereabouts; it was only a few kilometres away, he'd told us, and he would take us to it. But if Cheiron's cave was so close, why didn't Nikos know about it?

To add to the conundrum a book I'd just read about the local Pelion region mentioned Cheiron, claiming that his cave was at or near the village of Vizitsa beyond Milies in the centre of the eastern Pelion crab-claw region; yet the Archaeological Museum in Volos where we'd been the day before, informed us positively that Cheiron's cave was down south on the west side of the crab-claw peninsula at Milina. Harry, however, was not prepared to drive all that way for a cave (about eighty kilometres), especially since the symbol for a cave was not, repeat NOT, shown on any map. His attitude was that it didn't matter if we didn't see the 'wretched' cave. It was enough to know it existed, if it existed at all, scoff, scoff. Why couldn't I be satisfied with the cave Dimitri was taking us to later that afternoon, never mind if Nikos knew nothing about it.

I decided for the time being to say nothing more on the subject. Meanwhile we planned to drive to Chorefto, much further up this coast where I believed Achilles' parents, King Peleus and the sea-goddess Thetis had first met – in a cave.

★

We drove inland to join the main mountain road which would take us to the furthest coastal point in the north-east of the Pelion region. From the main road we took a secondary one for Zagoria and then zigzagged down to Chorefto on the coast. Before reaching Zagoria the scenery gradually unfurled from densely wooded mountain peaks and ravines to wide wooded valleys; here the mountains sloped towards each other, speckled here and there with small white-washed villages peeping from the trees.

We came to one of Mt. Pelion's many streams. Great glistening, silver-grey boulders were firmly wedged together up the mountainside, as though they had been professionally landscaped for the cascading water; tall plane trees flanked it. We stopped and climbed over the huge boulders. All around were wild flowers and aromatic herbs; Pelion was renowned for its plants with medicinal qualities. Cheiron had known them all as is evident when a wounded Greek warrior appealed to Patroclus for help: '*...see me safe to my black ship. I want you to cut out this arrow from my thigh, wash off the blood with warm water and spread soothing ointment on the wound. You have many excellent ones you learned from Achilles, who was taught by Cheiron, the most honest of the centaurs...*' (Iliad Bk11:828-833)

We sat on one of the glistening boulders and listened to the splash and ripple of the water. I thought about the centaurs; only Cheiron was a civilized centaur. Most were unruly, lustful creatures who took after their ancestor the wicked Ixion, king of the Lapiths. There was a story that Ixion had once developed a passion for Hera whom he had tried to rape. When Hera told her dear husband Zeus (who surely should know more than anyone what passion was) he was furious, and set a trap to catch Ixion out. He made a cloud in the image of his wife, and Ixion fell for it. Seeing what he thought was Hera, he ravished the cloud who consequently gave birth to a monstrous son named Centaurus; Centaurus in his turn mated with the wild mares of Mt. Pelion, and so these centaurs, half-man, half-horse, were born.

As for Ixion, Zeus, having caught him in the act of raping the cloud-come-Hera, punished him for eternity by tying him to a rotating fiery four-spoked wheel.

Though Ixion brought discredit on the Lapith people, they were in fact regarded as a civilized race. At the start of the Trojan War the Lapiths sent forty ships to join King Agamemnon's armada.

When we drove on we entered apple-orchard territory where farm trucks were being loaded up with crates of apples. It seemed appropriate for this area because it had been a golden apple that Eris (Strife) had thrown down amongst the wedding guests at Peleus and Thetis' wedding. She could have thrown down an orange or a lemon but, no, here on Mt. Pelion it had been an apple.

In due course we came down to Chorefto, and the sparkling blue Aegean sea. It looked idyllic from the car, but when we got out we were hit by a cold northerly gale. We set off briskly along the stretch of sandy beach towards a promontory. Long, low waves hurled themselves up the shore and, at the far end, the long, rocky outcrop was being pounded by the waves sending white spume spinning up into the air. I thought it reflected Patroclus' assessment of Achilles' character when he was refusing to fight and the Greeks were in grave danger. He accused Achilles of being pitiless and inhuman; he could not be the son of a mortal father or his divine mother '*...No, the grey sea and the sheer cliffs produced you and your unfeeling heart...*' (Iliad Bk16:35-36)

We'd come to this area because I knew that it had been the custom for Achilles' mother Thetis to rise from her grotto deep in the Aegean and come to a cave along this far north-eastern coastline.

The story goes that before her marriage both Zeus and Poseidon had been enamoured of her; but, because they knew that Fate had decreed that any son of hers would far surpass the greatness of the father, they had been wary of having anything to do with her. Hera, from long experience of her husband's extra-marital affairs, was none too keen on having this loose canon of an unattached virgin attracting the eye of her husband, and so she wanted her married off quickly. Since King Peleus was highly regarded by the gods, it was arranged that he should be the one to win her hand.

Peleus was informed about his bride-to-be, and was told to wait till the night of a full moon, and then to come to the cave where the beautiful sea-nymph was in the habit of coming up to the shore to dance with her sisters about the altar on which they, the daughters of Nereus, received offerings. Peleus was warned that, like her father Nereus, *silver-footed* Thetis when caught would change shape and do all she could to shake him off, and he must keep hold of her till eventually she would tire. So it was that somewhere along here Peleus spied Thetis and managed to wrestle her to the ground despite her transformation in turn from fire, to water, to a lion, a serpent – He clung on till she submitted, and they spent their first night together. It was the following day that the gods celebrated their marriage at a great gathering outside Cheiron's cave.

When we reached the rocky outcrop, we found the rocks spectacular in their variegated strata: hues of ginger, russet, cream, grey and green; we even thought we could detect patches of white marble. But we found no cave.

Harry spotted a notice-board with an arrow pointing along a pathway over the rocks to the next cove. We clambered up and walked for a while amongst shrubs and small trees as we headed for what from the far distance I took to be a lighthouse. But when we reached it on its rocky point it turned out to be a whitewashed stone shrine to the Virgin Mary. The wind whistled around us. From there we could see no cave in the next cove either. It seemed pointless to continue on this fruitless search.

My mind turned to Jason and the Argonauts who'd sailed up this coast on their quest for the Golden Fleece.

When at Volos we'd seen a replica of Jason's galley, the *Argo*, an amazing rustic looking vessel moored up and completely dwarfed beside a flashy white yacht. Harry had been captivated by this small replica.

Amongst the Argonauts had been Achilles' father Peleus. In one story Peleus had made the journey before his marriage because it was said that Thetis and her sisters had risen in wonder from the sea to watch it sailing by, and it was then that Peleus first spotted his future bride. In another Peleus was already married – the popular belief in that was Cheiron with his wife Chariclo had come down from his cave to the ancient port to see the Argonauts off, and he'd had the infant Achilles in his arms. Either story has its own charm.

We began the long walk back along the sandy shore to our car. The beach was almost deserted; there was only the odd makeshift hut or awning for shelter, created by a stalwart modern-day Achilles with his Patroclus, or his Briseis. The few young people we saw were acclimatized to the cold wind: the men were muscular and bare-chested, the girls wore sleeveless shifts and were bare-legged. Remnants of charred wood and ash showed where their meals were cooked; rolled up sleeping-bags and a homespun hammock made of plaited reeds strung between posts, revealed their sleeping habits. We passed a young man seated on a rickety looking chair strumming a guitar and humming quietly to himself. He could have been Achilles who, when an embassy from King Agamemnon arrived to propose the return of his beloved Briseis together with rich compensation (so desperate was the Greek army for his help at the time), was found *... taking his pleasure playing a clear-voiced lyre, a curious finely-worked instrument with a cross-piece of silver...He was delighting his soul, and singing the glories of heroes...* (Iliad Bk9:186-190)

We reached the car and took refuge in it out of the cold north wind. We were soon winding our way up over the mountains back to Agios Ioannis. We must not be late for Dimitri who was taking us to see HIS Cheiron's cave – the cave where the young Achilles grew up under the care of the wise centaur.

★

We followed the cream-coloured jeep ahead of us with Dimitri driving it and his friend Spiros beside him. We wound our way up the road heading for the village of Mouresi. Before reaching it the jeep drew up in a lay-by and we parked behind it. Spiros led the way and Dimitri took up the rear. We followed one of the Mt. Pelion ancient *kalderimia* partly hidden by undergrowth. These *kalderimia* were ancient cobbled tracks constructed originally to connect the mountain villages of Pelion.

We picked our way through the brambles before the track began to plummet steeply into a deep forested ravine. Having no head for heights I grabbed Dimitri's arm, and good-naturedly he allowed me to use him as an anchor as we went down. We had to make our way cautiously around the occasional boulder perched precariously on the precipice, and I averted my eyes from the autumn-leafed trees which stood rooted to the vertical descent. More dense forest rose up beyond and on either side.

Harry followed Spiros fairly sure-footedly with the help of his stick, pausing every now and then to look around. The sky was blue with puffs of white cloud.

On down and down and down through the autumnal gold and bronze-leafed mountain trees. After about four hundred metres we manoeuvred round to the right where there was a widish ledge. Spiros and Harry already stood beside dark grey boulders against which were what I took to be bright yellow autumn crocuses – I was to discover later they weren't crocuses but a species of amaryllis called *sternbergia lutea*. More importantly there was the cave – a great gaping hole in the ground over which was laid a cattle-grid-type covering to prevent anyone from falling into what looked like a bottomless cavity.

I hoped I didn't show any disappointment. After Nestor's cave at Pylos, it would be difficult to find another of the same ilk. Harry said: "There! That should satisfy my dear wife! Cheiron's cave! Now we can all go home!"

Dimitri and Spiros stood either side of it smiling expectantly, waiting for a show of enthusiasm from me.

"Amazing!" I said. I stared at it, and then at the plummeting forest beside us. A great cavity in the ground? It would be a major feat to clamber out, even if you were half-horse, or even all horse. It was said that Achilles' parents held their wedding outside Cheiron's cave and all the immortals were present together with their other guests. Where could they have possibly stood together? Or sat down? As Hera said to Apollo: '*...All you gods came to the wedding. And so did you, Apollo, and sat down at the wedding feast, lyre in hand...*' (Iliad Bk24:62-63)

But maybe the word 'outside' just meant it wasn't held 'inside'. It could as easily have been held anywhere 'outside' in some convenient glade or plateau like one in the mountains on the road to Volos which we'd seen the day before. Then I'd noticed a wide area of forest below the road like a shallow bowl; the autumn colours of the trees had been radiant in the sunshine with a thin stretch of vapour hanging over the area like a wedding-veil. It had a peculiar magic of its own and I'd thought at the time that there, surely, must be where the wedding had been celebrated.

It has been said that Thetis and Peleus had six sons before the birth of Achilles. But all six had perished as a result of Thetis trying to immortalize them by burning away their mortality. No wonder King Peleus had snatched the infant Achilles from his mother and placed him in the care of Cheiron!

"The cave is six hundred metres in depth," Dimitri said with pride as we gazed into the gaping mouth of it. A very large cave indeed. I took out my small torch and shone its feeble light into the formidable cavern but could only see darkness and rugged granite. Dimitri might call it Cheiron's cave but – well, I'd made a new discovery. After returning from Chorefto, I'd been looking at the various maps we had of the Mt. Pelion region, and had discovered on one of them the symbol of a cave at the village of Vizitsa. This confirmed what my book on the mythology of Mt. Pelion had said, that it was where Cheiron had lived. My spirits soared. Vizitsa – hmmm. How to get Harry there without mentioning the word 'cave'? I could suggest we explore the right-hand crab-claw of the Mt. Pelion region – I could just happen to notice the cave-symbol on the map and fake surprise when close to the village – I felt confident I could somehow swing it.

"That was quite wonderful!" I said to Dimitri when we'd made our hazardous way back up to the road. Dimitri looked delighted that he'd pleased his visitors so easily.

"Well, there you are!" Harry said contentedly, as we drove back to Agios Ioannis. "You've now done your Cheiron cave, thank the Lord!"

★

So here we are on our way to Vizitsa at the heart of Mt. Pelion. I have managed to keep off the taboo 'cave' subject with Harry. Well, I might have just touched on the word last night in a light staccato manner, or mentioned it this morning in a barely audible stage whisper. The main thing is that I've seen that horse-shoe symbol on the map denoting the dreaded word, and we are heading towards it.

On our way we stop at a village called Tsagarada for a thousand-year-old plane tree – this attraction has proved a very successful bait to get us closer to my goal. Harry paces out around the girth of the tree and announces it is an amazing twenty-three long strides; he then paces the extent of its branches and declares it is sixty-three strides. It is a playground for young children who pop in and out of the fork of its great branches; one of the branches is so long and heavy it is supported by a brick-built column.

A craft shop beckons and I find myself surrounded by articles made of local wood, and hand-made jewellery. It is a fatal error entering because I spy a silver-wrought bracelet set with garnets and I try it on. I am immediately captivated by it, and to my surprise and joy Harry says he'll buy it for me. He slightly pales at the price but doesn't shy away, and I wonder whether he has ulterior motives; as the driver he has control of the car and, therefore, the final say as to which direction to take. I am only the map-reader giving instructions. I don't want my secret plan to be scuppered – he too can be secretive and devious.

While he is busy counting out his euros, I try on a flamboyantly large silver-wrought ring just to see what it looks like on a finger; I am merely curious. Much to my dismay I am quite unable to get it off again. My finger swells as I struggle with the ring. The back of it is not a complete circle but has a gap, and I try to prise the two ends apart, whereupon one sharp end digs in and draws blood. Meanwhile, the young shop-keeper who tells us he is filling in for his father, hovers anxiously. I tell him that I need cold water and soap. Harry thinks I'm making a stupid exhibition of myself and says that he can get it off, but retires in utter confusion and terror because he realizes I appear to be lumbered with this ring I do not want, and he might have to pay for it also.

The young man reluctantly takes me into the clobber of the back premises and shows me a basin and a sliver of old soap. He's embarrassed, I'm embarrassed, Harry's embarrassed. I quickly run the cold water, apply the soap and, with a great deal of pulling and easing, I get the ring over the joint. Fortunately the ring is undamaged.

We are glad to drive on, and Harry is following my instructions. I think I've been unfair in suspecting his gift of a bracelet is a sweetner because he has scuppering intentions. In fact, he himself speaks the taboo word: "Do you know where your 'wretched' cave is exactly?"

Good God, he's suspected all along! Of course, after decades of marriage he knows my tactics only too well.

I say: "Well, no, not exactly. The horseshoe sign is sort of in the space over Vizitsa."

"You mean it could be anywhere?"

"Around the village."

"There's a lot of area around a village," Harry retorts.

When we reach Vizitsa, I ask at a small grocer's shop if they know the exact location of Cheiron's cave. The woman stares at me and says that any cave in the area – and there are many of them – is Cheiron's cave; the whole Pelion region is Cheiron's. She is sorry she cannot help, but it might be worth asking at the taverna. It is time to eat anyway, so we climb a cobbled path to the taverna which has extensive views out over the wooded slopes of a ravine to the distant sea. I ask the proprietor's wife if she knows of a Cheiron cave in the locality, and she gives me a sorrowful look; her husband knows, she says, but he is away till the following day.

I have one last attempt at finding out the whereabouts of this elusive cave; I home in on a young couple seated outside on the terrace. I have been watching them, and the man has been trying for at least half an hour to cheer up his female companion. All the while she has been looking sullen and totally fed up with him.

I approach their table and ask if they are familiar with the area, and if by any chance they know… I smile at them encouragingly. The girl, who has long dark hair, comes a little to life at this interruption, and her beauty shows briefly; but she says she's sorry she has no idea. Her face blanks out immediately as she turns back to her companion who shrugs and says he's never heard of it. When I return to Harry and glance their way again, I see they have fallen back into their sullen and don't-know-what-to-do-about-it state.

By now I feel the whole Cheiron thing lies in the lap of the gods. If it is destined we are to find it, then Fate will lead us to it. All we need do is to start walking.

With this Fate idea in mind Harry and I follow a *kalderimi*. We pass dogs barking and chickens clucking, and gradually descend a ravine; the cobbled track is flanked by clumps of wild flowers and dried herbs. Cheiron, of course, was well informed about juices extracted from the roots and stems, and the curative remedies of the leaves and petals of every plant we see.

We descend the track for about a mile but then baulk at the even steeper descent and the fact that what goes down needs to be climbed back up. So we sit down at a vantage point and gaze out across the ravine where we can see a rockface rising to a dirt road.

"There you are – a cave!" Harry announces. I look towards where Harry is pointing. It might be a cave, and it might as easily not be one either, a mere shadow. I have no desire to go blindly on depending on Fate to lead us to it.

"Maybe," I say. I am becoming indifferent about it – yes, I'm ashamed that by now even I am beginning to regard it as a 'wretched' cave, a complete bother.

I use my thumb-nail to detach a dried-out stalk of a miniature flowering plant whose leaves when crushed have a pungent smell, then hand it to Harry to sniff; he puts it to one nostril, then the other, but he can't identify it.

I turn my attention to the view and the distant sea. I think it must be the Pagasitikos gulf where ancient Pegasae had been and the old port of Iolchos on the outskirts of Volos were located. When in Volos we'd tried to get to Pegasae but without success. With frayed tempers we'd headed in the wrong direction caught up in a traffic flow with no easy means of turning round.

It had been to Iolchos that King Nestor and Odysseus had come to recruit men from Mt. Pelion to join King Agamemnon's forces. King Pelius had agreed to send fifty ships under the leadership of young Achilles, and had equipped him with three of his most treasured possessions: his magnificent suit of armour, and the two immortal horses, Xanthus and Balius – wedding-gifts from the gods; and Cheiron's spear with a handle made of manna ash from the Mt. Pelion region (also a wedding-gift).

At the outset of the war Achilles had been only fifteen so Peleus had appointed his trusted friend Phoenix to be Achilles' lieutenant, his guardian and adviser. When, ten years later, Achilles had been in his prolonged sulk over his stolen slave-girl and was threatening to sail home, Phoenix had tried to reason with him: ... *'Glorious Achilles,... if you really are pondering departure in your heart, because of your obsessive anger and you refuse to save the gallant ships from going up in flames, what is to become of me without you, my dear boy?... Peleus, when he sent you off from Phthia to join Agamemnon, made me your guardian. You were only a youth, with no experience of the dangers of war, nor of public speaking, where people make their mark. It was to teach you all these things, to make a persuasive speaker of you and a man of action, that he sent me to accompany you...'* (Iliad Bk9:434-443)

He warned Achilles not to lose the respect of the Greek army, to which Achilles replied stubbornly: *'...I find it unseemly that you favour lord Agamemnon and thereby upset me with a display of such emotion. Be careful not to wish to please him, or you may change my love for you to hate. The right thing for you to do is to show contempt for the man who shows contempt for me...'* (Iliad Bk9:612-616)

That Achilles sailed with the Myrmidons from Iolchos was at odds with the other story that his mother Thetis, knowing that Achilles was destined to die in the war, spirited him away to the island of Skyros disguised as a girl. There he'd lived in the women's quarters at the king's palace, where he'd been discovered by Odysseus who must have been told where he was in hiding. He was aware that the war could not be won without him, and came with jewellery for the girls. He showed them the necklaces and rings, but also placed a weapon amongst them, whereupon the disguised Achilles promptly revealed his identity by going for the weapon.

Whilst on Skyros Achilles had got the king's daughter pregnant and his son Neoptolemus had been born. It was Neoptolemus who'd played a major and ruthless part in the final destruction of Troy; he'd entered the palace when Troy was burning, and was *a figure of armed insolence*. Seeing the elderly King Priam tremulously trying to put on his armour Neoptolemus, blind with rage and blood-lust, ... *dragged Priam, quaking and sliding in a pool of his own son's blood* (a son named Polites)...*twined his left hand in Priam's hair... and brutally slaughtered him.*

It seems shocking to be pondering these painful, cataclysmic thoughts whilst seated in such tranquil and peaceful surroundings. I return to thinking of Achilles, not his son; Achilles at least had a modicum of pity in his heart when King Priam came to his hut and clasped his knees in supplication, pleading for the return of his son Hector's body. Then the great Achilles had treated King Priam with gentleness and kindness. They'd sat down to a meal together, each respecting the other despite the tragedy of war. Little did he know then that his pitiless son Neoptolemus was to kill Priam in such a brutal manner following his own death. Achilles' death had finally come about by an arrow in his heel fired by Paris and directed by Apollo, though those final days of the war weren't in the *Iliad* but in the *Aeneid*.

By now the sun is lower in the sky, and has gone behind a mountain peak; it is getting rapidly cooler here where we are seated. We get up from our boulder, and begin the long climb back up, past the clucking hens and barking dogs; the scene is far removed from the raging fires, crashing buildings, and the screams of dying men and women that have filled my mind.

It is Sunday and we are seated in a seventeenth century church in a village called Kissos. We've been told this church is well worth seeing, and the fact that it is Sunday is not a sudden holiness on our part, but curiosity. It is an unusual building with four interior domes, though they are not visible from the outside. It was built during the Turkish occupation and, therefore, its exterior had to be inconspicuous and lower than any mosque. Its long, gently sloping roof is covered with the grey fish-scale tiles typical of the Pelion region. The church building is surrounded by a large paved area and, from the outside, it is unspectacular. It could be taken for a school. In fact, under the Turks it was secretly used for just that.

Seated here inside is like being in a jewel-box. The *iconostasis* is the most spectacularly carved and gilded sancturary screen I've ever seen, with numerous icons of the saints. Hanging before it is a lighted chandelier of brilliant crystal drops; ropes of looped crystal have been gathered together to a point and finished off with a dark blue boss.

The church is dedicated to Agia Marina, a third century fifteen-year-old girl who was tortured and persecuted but refused to abandon her Christian beliefs. The pagan gods who had watched over the Greeks and Trojans during that ten-year war were to her an abomination, a wild figment of man's imagination.

Today people pray to God, or beseech God's one and only Son who gave his life to save us from our sins – something I have never understood, the save us from our sins part. Under the pagan gods men had given their lives because of men's sins; many had died for no reason other than the sins of Helen. Patroclus was yet another who'd given his life as a result of Achilles' unrelenting fury with Agamemnon who'd stolen his slave-girl. In the *Iliad* Patroclus accuses him: '*…you are impossible. God preserve me from the bitterness you harbour! You and your disastrous greatness – what will future generations have to thank you for, if you do nothing to prevent the Greeks' humiliating destruction? You are quite pitiless…*' (Iliad Bk16:30-34)

When Patroclus died, and Achilles realized that it was due to his own futile fury and pride, his sense of guilt overwhelmed him. Even in sleep he was haunted. Patroclus came to him in a dream demanding a swift burial: '*…For I have been swallowed up by the dreadful doom that must have been my lot from birth; and it is your destiny too, godlike Achilles, to perish under the rich Trojans' walls.*

*'Something else now, one more request. Do not let them bury my bones apart from yours, Achilles. Let them lie together, just as you and I grew up together in your house…let the one container, the golden two-handled vessel your lady mother gave you, hold our bones.*' (Iliad Bk23:79-92)

As I sit in this magnificent old church I ponder how Patroclus had sacrificed his life for his friend Achilles. I remember the words of a Canon when for some reason we were talking about death and funerals. He had said something I have never forgotten, that for those left behind there was often a sense of guilt, and that was the main thing he found he had to address when dealing with bereaved families.

Harry's voice startles me out of my thoughts. "Are you finished in here?" He has clearly had enough of the small church's beauty. Reluctantly I leave, and we go out to the surrounding terrace where another huge old plane tree stands spreading its branches and offering shade.

A man and woman are examining the tree and we get into conversation with them; both enthuse about the church and the tree. For some reason I have got into my head that the *iconostasis* in the church has been carved from the manna ash, the same wood which I believe constructed the *Argo* (I must have read it somewhere). I am interested in the manna ash because Homer specifically mentions that Cheiron gave Achilles' father the manna ash-handled spear as a wedding-present, and Peleus had handed it on to Achilles. The manna ash grows on Mt. Pelion, but where is, or what is, the manna ash? We haven't seen any ash trees amongst the numerous different species on the forested slopes.

I ask the couple now if they have come across this tree. The man is interested and has an ipad. With great gusto he taps in the letters and up comes an image of the tree. Its leaves are nothing like the British ash, but are similar to those of a beech tree; its trunk also is grey like a beech, but it is tall and slender. The man discovers from his ipad that the tree grows in abundance a few kilometres further north from Kissos where we are.

Kissos is a unique and attractive village which rises up the mountainside from the church. We decide to look for the manna ash, and then return for lunch. Secretly I wonder if Kissos has a cave; the immortal wedding guests could have gathered here on the levelled area where the church now stands.

In less than ten minutes we come suddenly to the manna ash forest. They are unmistakable with their tall and slender trunks – perfect for carving the pillars of the *iconostasis* in the church, or for the construction of a galley like the *Argo*. It wasn't till I'd returned home that, in fact, I discovered the manna ash hadn't been used for either the *Argo* or the *iconostasis*.

But I am pleased we have discovered the tree because of the ash-handled spear. Homer describes it as a massive and heavy weapon which only Peleus was able to use before Achilles. Patroclus hadn't taken it when he'd gone into battle because Achilles knew he'd be unable to wield it. When, though, Patroclus was killed, and he himself had taken up arms intent on slaughtering Hector to avenge his friend's death, Achilles had armed himself with it: *...he took his father's spear from its case, long, thick and heavy that no Greek could wield and only he knew how to handle it. It was made from a Mount Pelion ash and had been given to his father, Peleus, by Cheiron, to bring death to his noble foes...* (Iliad Bk19:386-391)

Before killing Hector with it, Achilles went on the rampage hacking down as many Trojans as he could. Amongst those killed was one named Asteropaeus: *...Now Achilles...hurled his ash shaft at Asteropaeus intending to kill him, but missed and struck the high riverbank with such force that he buried half the length of the ash spear in it. Drawing his sharp sword from his side, the son of Peleus charged at Asteropaeus, who was now trying in vain to drag the ash spear out from the bank with his great hand. Three times, in his attempts to retrieve the spear, he shifted it a little, but each time he had to give up the struggle. He tried again, this time to bend and break the ash shaft, but before he could do so, Achilles was on him and killed him with his sword...* (Iliad Bk21:169-180)

We begin to walk along a muddy track amongst the tall manna ash trees, but then find the path roped off with a warning sign. We have no good reason to go further and it is particularly cold that day; the thought of hot food beckons us.

We return to Kissos and find a taverna up the slope behind the church where an old man is seated outside watching the world go by. Inside a log-fire blazes in a wood-burning stove. On one wall are family photographs, and beside them is the skin of a wild boar fastened to the wall. The young waitress, who we are to discover is a psychology student at university and only working in the family taverna over the vacation, tells us that her grandfather (the old man seated outside) had shot it. There are many wild boar in the mountains, she says, and at this time of year they live on chestnuts. The village would be overrun with them if they were not regularly culled.

While under Cheiron's care the young Achilles had been fed on wild boar together with the offal of lions, and the marrow of bears to help him grow strong and courageous; he was also given the marrow of fawns and fed on honey-combs to ensure he ran faster than any other human. According to Robert Graves in his *Greek Myths*, Achilles was only six years old when he killed his first wild boar, and he was so fleet of foot that he could outrun and kill a stag.

There is a photo of Grandpapa on the taverna wall, rifle over one arm and holding up his prize wild boar. But before firearms were invented it was a feat indeed to corner and kill the wild animals of the mountains. For Achilles to have lived his early life under the care of the centaur Cheiron, half-man, half-horse, who must himself have had the speed of a horse – or half a horse, as Harry put it, since only his hind-legs were equine – must have given the child Achilles the belief that he too could keep up with or outrun his foster father.

For us, however, it is time to leave. It is sad, because tomorrow we have to depart from Mt. Pelion and return to Thessaloniki for our flight the following day. Pelion is an area of Greece like no other; it is uniquely itself. One day I hope that we'll return.

★

We have driven to Makrinitsa since it's more or less on our way. Makrinitsa is known as the 'balcony' of Mt. Pelion, because it clings to the mountainside and overlooks the Pagasitikos gulf. The pedestrianised centre is lined with small shops selling produce from the mountains – herbs and jars of jam, chestnuts, apple jelly, honey – It is very tempting to go away armed with unnecessary treats and might-be-needed-remedies for heart-burn, liver problems, kidney-stones, you name it, they have it. But Harry hauls me away and marches me up a narrow road to a monastery on a higher level – if we were in a theatre you might say we had left the stalls and had climbed up to the gods. There we sit with a bird's eye view to the sea, scanning the crab's claw for a sighting of Pegasae, the ancient Bronze Age site.

I imagine King Peleus seeing off Achilles aged fifteen, primed and ready for battle thanks to the attentive tutoring and athletic training given him by Cheiron. And with him is his guardian Phoenix, sent by Peleus to advise and keep an eye on his impetuous son – not that he could influence or reason with him when he was at his most obdurate. With him too is his beloved childhood companion Patroclus. Little do any of them know that they are never to return.

But today the sun still shines; the sea continues to sparkle; and, although more than three thousand years have passed, their story is remembered. As Achilles himself said: '*...My divine mother, Thetis of the silver-feet, says that Fate has prepared two courses open to me as I journey to the grave. If I remain and join with others in attacking Troy, there is no home-coming for me, though I will win undying fame and glory...*' (Iliad Bk9:410-413)

The alternative was to return home early and live a long and uneventful life. How much more interesting for the world that he chose glory.

# OLYMPUS, THE MOUNTAIN OF THE GODS

The name Olympus comes from the Greek words 'oly' (all) and 'lambos' (shining) – 'all-shining'. It conjures up a picture of Homer's glittering gold palaces of the immortal gods. In reality, the higher reaches of this great mountain are grey shale and rugged rocky peaks.

Mt. Olympus is awesome and majestic, densely forested with here and there deep ravines, boulder-strewn gorges and swift-flowing crystal clear streams feeding the main river Enipeus. The Mytikas is the highest point at nine thousand, five hundred and seventy feet above sea-level. Just below the summit is the Throne of Zeus, a lofty, scallop-shaped rock, a suitable regal seat for the indomitable lord of the heavens.

It is generally accepted there were twelve Olympian gods, nine of whom, according to Homer, played a part in the Trojan War. They were divided in their loyalties and often quarrelled furiously amongst themselves. But they also knew how to feast and relax and listen to Apollo on the lyre. The mountain has an aura of the divine about it; it has a feel of majesty and strength.

To this day Mt. Olympus remains a dominant and powerful presence rising from the landscape in north-east Thessaly, with the Aegean sea extending out to the east as a broad and sparkling blue band separating the Greek mainland from the Trojan shores.

CHAPTER

# 8

# MT. OLYMPUS

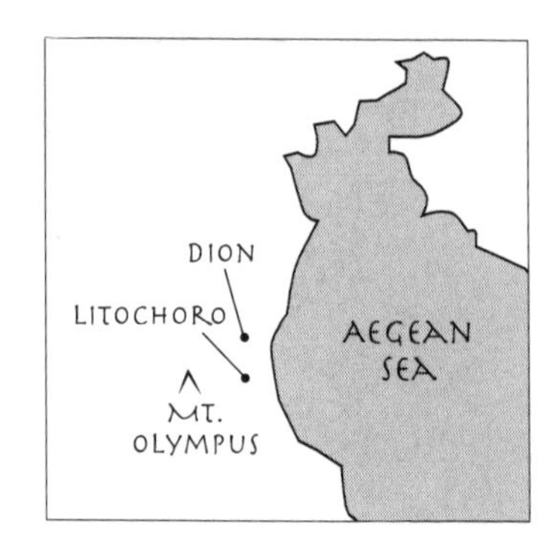


No one driving along the motorway where the Mt. Olympus massif rises from the flat Thessalian plain can fail to be impressed by it. On our way I noticed that its silhouetted outline against the skyline was not a straight up and down curve, but sloped with gentle upward thrusts which, with imagination, could be seen as chariots swooping down Olympus driven by the immortals. Fanciful, no doubt, but I was viewing the craggy peaks from the perspective of those ancients who first conjured up the stories of the gods intervening in the Trojan War.

When we eventually arrived at Litochoro, the picturesque town at the foot of Mt. Olympus, and were installed in our hotel (picked because it promised views to the mountain), we found that it surpassed all expectation. From where we sat out on our balcony that evening, the distant wide and forested bulk of the mountain had several central craggy peaks streaked with crevices of snow which soared spectacularly to the heavens. There before us was the home of the Olympian gods.

In the foreground, which I thought significant, and not twenty metres away from our hotel, was a church with a gabled roof on top of which was a shining cross silently proclaiming Christianity to the world.

I stared out at the mountain, then looked again at the nearby church. It was astonishing that visitors from all over the world came to Litochoro because they'd been inspired by Homer's *Iliad* whose words had heightened their awareness of the pagan deities from more than three millennia ago; it was thought then that the gods responded to the needs of men, though only if they sacrificed and poured libations in their turn to them – it was a reciprocal unwritten understanding between the seen and unseen; an awareness amongst men that there was an invisible presence greater and more powerful than themselves that needed to be recognized and honoured.

Later, as the sun was setting, we saw against the cloudless azure-amber sky, a single fine, thin line of a brightly gleaming vapour-trail left behind by a passenger jet, though the plane itself was not visible to the naked eye; the gleaming line moved slowly from west to east, from the mountain of the gods heading for Troy. It put me in mind of the occasion when the goddess Athena *...sped down from the peaks of Olympus, like a meteor that is sent by Zeus as a danger signal to mariners or some strong army on land, and comes streaking through the sky...* (Iliad Bk4:74-77)

The following day we drove the fifteen or so kilometres to Prionia, and parked our car at the trail-head. Prionia is a pine-built shop and café from which hikers aiming for the summit of Olympus stock up before setting off, or else refresh themselves on arriving down.

Our trek on this our first day was a short one, a mere limbering up after our long journey. The narrow path took us through the lower forest of beech, plane, and numerous deciduous trees punctured here and there by conifers. On this occasion we went no further than a forest glade where mules were grazing. Our attention was first drawn to them by the sound of a melodious, low-toned bell. From the track we could glimpse them through the trees, and could see that they had saddle-packs; they were, no doubt, waiting to be loaded with provisions to be taken to the Spilios Agapitos refuge-hut three-quarters of the way up to the summit.

We returned down to Prionia, and found a half concealed track descending to a gorge where a long chute of water cascaded down the cleft of a rockface, then widened to become a waterfall, all the more spectacular because it tumbled over slate-grey rock.

We perched ourselves on boulders beside a clear-as-crystal aquamarine rock-pool; we were partly in the sun, partly in dappled shade cast by overhanging branches.

I took off my sandals and dipped a bare foot into the water; but it was so icy-cold it made me yelp and I quickly withdrew it.

The indomitable, physical presence of the mountain here was overwhelming; it was both inviting and forbidding; it was soaring crags and deep ravines; it drew you on yet warned you off. It was inhabited by the gods, and you felt their presence everywhere. Certainly, here on Mt. Olympus the power of Zeus was reflected in the mountain peaks; yet Zeus was not always a dominating, angry god flinging thunderbolts, he could also be kindly disposed and affectionate.

For example, when Aphrodite had been wounded on the palm of her hand by Diomedes *...troubled by her pain, with her lovely skin covered with blood* (I thought the gods only had ichor) *Aphrodite withdew; the wound was stinging grievously; but Iris with feet as swift as the wind took over and led her from the battlefield...* (Iliad Bk5:353-356)

Aphrodite found Ares and implored him to lend her his chariot to take her back to Mt. Olympus. This he did, and when she reached Olympus, she found her mother Dione who *...took her daughter in her arms and stroked her with her hand, speaking to her fondly: 'Dear child, which of the gods of heaven has hurt you in this wanton manner as though you had done wrong...?'*

Laughter-loving Aphrodite answered her... She told her how it had been Diomedes, and her mother soothed her, listing the many wounds that had been suffered by the gods at the hands of men. She then *...wiped the ichor from Aphrodite's hand with both her own. The wound healed, and the dreadful smarting was drawn from the pain...* (Iliad Bk5:370-419)

Aphrodite's distress hadn't gone unnoticed by Hera and Athena who taunted her mercilessly (after all, she supported the enemy). They scoffed at the slight wound, suggesting it was only a scratch from a brooch worn by one of Aphrodite's love-struck women victims. Zeus heard them and it *...drew a smile from the father of men and gods. But he called golden Aphrodite to him and said: 'Warfare, my child, is not for you. You are in charge of marriage and passion. We will leave Ares and Athena to look after military matters.'...* (Iliad Bk5:427-431)

On another occasion when all the immortals had re-entered the war, each supporting their favoured side, Artemis received rough treatment from Hera, and thoroughly distraught she rushed back to Olympus and *...weeping sat herself on her father's knee, while round her her divine robe quivered. The son of Kronos took her to him, laughing gently: 'Dear child of mine, which of the heavenly gods has treated you like this?'...* (Iliad Bk21:504 509)

Such unseen activity here on the mountain! Those invisible gods metamorphosed into exaggerated human form with human thoughts and feelings! The early Christian Fathers had been scornful, saying that the gods were nothing more than mere poetic fancy. Yet at the time of Homer they were as real as those who believe intuitively in God today.

While thinking these thoughts I examined a wild geranium growing from a crack in the boulder at my feet. Behind me higher up was a fir which had seeded itself in a crevice in the rockface and was sending out three or four straggly pine-needled branches.

I wondered how a young fellow named Nicagoras was getting on. We'd met him and his girlfriend Liziana at breakfast that morning and had got into conversation with them. They were about to tackle the mountain, and hoped to climb up to the peak tomorrow after sleeping in the refuge-hut tonight.

"Nicagoras," I said, "I wonder how he's doing?"

"Well, I don't suppose he's thinking 'gods'," Harry remarked dismissivly.

Nicagoras was Greek. He had strong features and clear brown eyes which fixed intently on whoever he was speaking to. He had very positive disbeliefs, and was completely frank about what he thought regarding his own and our views. There was a refreshing honesty about him. Surprisingly, he spoke very good English though in every sentence he used the 'f' word to which each time I interrupted with a 'Shhhh!' His girlfriend sat smiling tolerantly, and wisely said little unless Nicagoras turned to her and asked for her opinion.

"You write about how Christianity took over from the f…ing gods? Pah!" And his expression said it all: a mild contempt but also curiosity. "You don't believe in all that f…ing nonsense?"

I rose to the occasion. "You can't NOT believe in anything," I said.

Our conversation had been intense and concentrated. He had read Christopher Hitchens and Richard Dawkins, and was a confirmed atheist. On all such occasions I inevitably argue that there is something other than what can be seen; there is an energy, a power, a something-or-another which is (maybe) guiding, is (maybe) guarding, is (maybe) helping you fulfil your destiny.

When Harry had ventured to say that there was nothing wrong with Christianity, and it was better to believe in something than nothing, Nicagoras said emphatically: "Pah! You can't f…ing believe what a man in a black cap and long black robe tells you? Why the f… would you want to believe those fantasies?"

The more I said 'Shhhhh!' the more he enjoyed provoking me with the 'f' word, and the more Liziana smiled patiently.

"I'm always saying to my wife," Harry remarked, "that it's better to go along with Christianity just in case it's true. When you die there's no second chance!"

I found that thought alarming. No second chance? But was it true in the first place, this hell and damnation belief? One could never be sure! But Nicagoras raised his arms in despair at the folly of it all. The discussion had lasted without pause for more than an hour. We had followed their car to Prionia, and had walked a little way up the track with them, before they'd continued on alone; their intention being – as was the intention of most climbers – to reach the summit the next morning.

I found it difficult to let go the fact that I'd never reached the summit myself. Harry thought it was of no consequence one way or another, but I hated defeat.

On our first trip to Greece many years ago we'd attempted to get up to the Mytikas peak to see the Throne of Zeus. We'd spent the night in the refuge-hut but had failed to reach our goal next day because Harry's back had seized up in the night – there was no question of Harry getting higher, but rather whether he could get lower. I was ashamed at how relieved I'd felt as I'd barely slept and, each time I'd managed to drop off I'd woken with a start dreaming I was falling down a precipice. A ridge along the summit, so I'd read and had been warned, was where vertigo could set in, and the thought haunted me. The next occasion (when Harry wasn't with me) I'd woken to dense white fog on the mountain, and worse weather was forecast. How relieved I'd felt again!

There were things to be said for being well advanced in years as now we weren't expected to climb anywhere. Instead, I could leave it to my imagination to take me where I wanted without stress or effort. Nevertheless, it was annoying that I'd failed in what had always been a firm ambition.

For this trip I'd thought of hiring a mule (visualizing myself as an intrepid adventurer), but that idea had been shot down promptly when Harry'd said that for me to sit astride a mule hour after hour – at my age – would leave me for ever walking (if I could ever walk again) with my legs bowed and bent as though astride a beast.

I'd then thought that hovering over the mountain in a helicopter might be the answer. I'd made enquiries but found the cost so exorbitant I dared not mention it aloud. Nevertheless, I'd kept returning to the idea; I'd imagined being harnessed up and lowered to the summit on a rope; I could sign my name in the visitor's book (as though I'd climbed the mountain), spend five minutes gazing all around before being winched back up and flying effortlessly away again.

And so my thoughts swung around my head to these opposite extremes – to do that summit come what may while we were here, or to let the opportunity pass and for ever live with the regret – to enjoy glorious victory, or suffer frustration and defeat –

In the same way Zeus also swung to extremes of opposing thoughts – of helping the Trojans, or witholding his assistance; of forbidding his family's involvement and then encouraging them to intervene. In a forbidding tone he warned them:

*'Listen to me, all you gods and goddesses, while I tell you what my heart within me has decided... Whatever you do, do not defy or disobey my order – you must accept it, each one of you. If I perceive any god going his own way and supporting the Trojans or the Greeks, he shall be thrashed and... I will... cast him into misty Tartarus, far away, where is the deepest gulf beneath the earth, where are the iron gates, and the bronze threshold, as far below Hades as heaven is above the earth. Then shall he know how far I am mightiest of all the immortals...'*

*Zeus finished, and they were all startled. He had spoken with tremendous force and left them dumbfounded...* (Iliad Bk8:5-17, 28-30)

When, however, Achilles was back on the battlefield, Zeus swung to the opposite extreme, and ordered all the gods to assemble. ... *They all gathered within the doors of the cloud-gatherer's palace; nor was the earthshaker Poseidon heedless... but from the salt sea came up after the rest, and sat himself amongst them, and enquired concerning the purpose of Zeus...*

*And Zeus who marshals the clouds answered him, saying: 'Earthshaker, you know why I have summoned you all here... I now give you all permission to join with the Trojans and the Greeks and give help to either side, as your sympathies dictate...* (Iliad Bk20:10-16,19-26)

Here in the gorge, the chute and waterfall were a constant all-enveloping sound as if we were seated in an auditorium, and surrounded by prolonged applause from an appreciative audience. Perhaps the gods were giving us a standing ovation for flying all the way from England, then driving overland to this their home? I could imagine them seated high up keeping an eye on us perched here on our boulders. If so, they were watching Harry opening his haversack and taking out our picnic lunch: rolls and cheese, and large tomatoes and plump ripe cherries. Harry set it out beside me; it was not exactly ambrosia, the food of the gods, nor was the water we drank nectar, but it was the food and drink we mortals had while seated on their mountain.

I noticed a couple walking on the rustic pinewood bridge that crossed the gorge; midway along, they paused and looked our way; they saw us by our aquamarine rock-pool and the cascading waterfall. I could imagine them (they were now pointing in our direction) discussing how they too could find their way here. Well, they only had to cross the bridge to find the partly hidden track that brought us down. We hoped, however, that our solitude would not be disturbed. We didn't want other humans coming, only the unseen and silent gods were welcome.

★

As we left our taverna late that evening we could see the sky over the mountain changing to a colour-wash of sepia as though it had been spilled across the heavens by an unseen hand. We hurried back to our hotel and, from our balcony, watched the gathering gloom as the wind got up, and ominous black clouds obliterated the mountain before rolling on relentlessly towards us. We could hear the distant thunder getting louder.

We wondered how Nicagoras and Liziana were up there in the refuge-hut enfolded in the storm with the thunder and lightning zigzagging from the heavens. It brought Zeus, the cloud gatherer and thrower of thunderbolts, vividly to life; it was the Trojan War at its peak.

A streak of forked lightning lit up the town, there was a terrific clap of thunder and the nearby church which had been floodlit suddenly blacked out. A minute later our lights also failed. Fortunately, I knew where our torch was and was able to feel my way to it. Not long afterwards there was a loud knocking at our door and, without waiting for an answer, the receptionist came in with a lantern-torch and placed it on our table. With nods and smiles she quickly withdrew.

The storm passed on, the rain eased, and soon the church was once again floodlit, its cross glistening against the night sky. Eventually our lights also came on and we were rudely brought back into the twenty-first century by the glare of electricity.

★

The following day was a fine, clear morning with a pallid half moon hanging in the sky. Like after a sudden, fierce marital argument, the storm of the night before was quickly forgotten. Instead, the first shafts of sunlight illuminated the rocky mountain peaks. Two wisps of pink-tinged cloud wafted peacefully above the crags. All was tranquil on the mountain this fine morning.

The day was set aside to visit Dion, a nearby archaeological site which we'd been to many years ago, but then my focus had been on how Christianity had won over from the pagan gods; this time I wanted to experience Dion with the *Iliad* in mind.

It's possible to tramp miles at Dion as it covers a vast plain. For those who love historical ruins it's an archaeological paradise. I myself have only one ruin I must see: the all-important sanctuary of Zeus which existed before the city was founded. The Greek word Dion means 'of Zeus' hence the city's name.

Because we have no steps or hills to climb, and ambling along flat paths is monotonously undemanding, I lead Harry to the wrong sanctuary, though the mistake, perhaps, is worth it. We stray over several wooden bridges across streams, passing through a jungle-like area of trees and shrubs where there are many butterflies and what we've been told by another interested spectator are damselflies; the latter flutter like butterflies, though they are similar in size and shape to dragonflies having the same thin bodies and thin wings which are of the darkest blue-black colour; their wings, unlike the dragon-fly, fold back like a butterfly when they settle down to rest. Harry spends at least five minutes staring at one settled on a leaf less than a foot away.

Emerging at last from this jungle-like area, we arrive at a sanctuary (not the one we want), but the temple of Zeus Hypsistos (Zeus 'the highest') of a later date. A notice tells us there was once a Sacred Way to it lined with columns topped by eagles, an important symbol of Zeus; and the sanctuary's cult statue was of Zeus holding a thunderbolt in one hand and a sceptre in the other.

But this is not the sanctuary I want and, after enquiries, we retrace our steps through the jungle area and across the streams to the comparatively treeless flat plain. At last we find the several blocks of stone outlining the early sanctuary of Zeus that I've been looking for. The dramatic backdrop to this ancient site is the impressive Mt.

Olympus massif which looms large, and we can see many more soaring peaks on this its north-east face.

I have come here because this is where Alexander the Great once honoured the supreme god of the ancient world with prayers and sacrifice before setting out on his campaigns. It is said that Alexander had had a great love of the *Iliad* and always carried a copy of it on his travels; when he slept he'd kept it along with his dagger beneath his head.

As a boy Alexander'd had none other than the renowned philosopher Aristotle for his tutor. It had been he who had introduced him to the *Iliad*, and his young pupil had been so inspired by this epic poem that he'd read it through at just one sitting, or so it was claimed. From then on Achilles became his hero, and the young Alexander was determined to be as fearless and indomitable in battle as Achilles had been; to stand up for what he thought was right against overwhelming opposition; and, as Achilles had with Patroclus, he'd developed a homosexual love for his childhood companion and fellow pupil Hephaistion. Unlike Achilles, though, who'd been able to avenge the death of his beloved Patroclus by pursuing and killing Hector, when Hephaistion died quite suddenly after a long fever, Alexander had no human foe to vent his grief and anger on; the shock to him of his beloved Hephaistion's unexpected death, caused Alexander such an all-consuming, uncontrollable grief that had lasted so long, his friends and colleagues had become seriously concerned.

I tell Harry what I think will interest him. "Do you know," I say, "that when Alexander the Great set out to conquer the world, he went to Troy?"

Harry's attention is immediately arrested and a cherry he is about to eat remains poised mid-way to his mouth. I tell him about Alexander's hero-worship of Achilles. "And, apparently," I continue, "when Alexander sailed in to Beşik bay, he cast his dagger deep into the sand to claim the territory as his own."

"Oh, yes? Whose territory was it then?" Harry asks.

"The Persians – I think," I answer.

"Hum."

"He then stripped off and, together with his beloved companion Hephaistion, whom he regarded as his Patroclus, ran naked around the tumulus which he believed was the one Achilles built for Patroclus, and where their bones had been laid together in death. The tumulus must have been the one we climbed, remember?"

"Why in heaven's name did he want to run naked around it?" Harry asks, dipping his hand into the bag of cherries and taking several more. I can give no answer. Instead I tell him how afterwards he'd gone up to Troy, which by then had been rebuilt as a village, and had visited the temple of Athena. There he'd been shown trophies from the Trojan War which included armour.

"And he thought it was Achilles'?" Harry enquires.

"Yes, as a matter of fact. And so he left his own armour there and took what he regarded was his hero's."

"The armour made by Heffy-thingummy?" Harry raises another cherry to his mouth and leaves it poised there waiting for my answer.

"Presumably."

He bites the cherry off its stalk, and chews it silently for a moment before spitting out the stone.

"It may be that Alexander's hero-worship of Achilles had something to do with his mother who was descended from Achilles," I say.

"Is that fact or fiction?" Harry asks; there is a touch of scepticism to his question.

"Well, according to Plutarch she was descended through Neoptolemus, Achilles' son."

"Hum."

After I take a share of cherries before they all disappear, I also tell him that it was here on this flat plain that Alexander, when only twelve years old, impressed his elders by his perception, resourcefulness and courage when he'd mounted and controlled an unschooled and impossibly excitable stallion no one else could handle. He had been watching the high-spirited beast's nervous antics, and had soon realized that the stallion kept shying away from its own shadow. Bearing this in mind, and keeping the sun in front, Alexander had soon leapt astride the animal and had it cantering obediently along the plain, while his proud father proclaimed with some accuracy that Macedonia would never be large enough to contain such a son when he grew up. From then on the stallion and Alexander had become inseperable, and it accompanied him on all his journeys. He might well have identified his beautiful Bucophalus (the stallion's name) with Achilles' immortal horses, Xanthus and Balius, who had the gift of speech and who'd shed 'hot tears' at the death of Patroclus.

"By the way, that damselfly," Harry unexpectedly remarks. I look at my dear husband whose mind has gone off-track somewhat. "I peered right into its two tiny pin-head black eyes from less than a foot away, and it was staring right back at me. I wonder what it was thinking?"

I play along with his new topic: "Maybe it thought you were a god?" I say.

"And between its pin-head eyes it had a pin-head turquoise nose."

"Or maybe you were so close your features merged into one large eye and it thought you were a Cyclops?" I suggest.

"And a tiny turquoise neck. Its colouring was really quite something! Brave little creature staring me in the eye like that," he remarks.

As he spits out a cherry-stone, he seems to wake up from what can only be described as a temporary lapse and trance-like diversion, and says: "So, are you finished here? Time for the sea and my swim?" He's suddenly impatient to be gone.

Having seen what I have come for, we return the way we came in, paying a brief visit to the recently reconstructed open-air theatre. On our former visit several decades earlier, the ancient theatre had been only a few insignificant tiered seats constructed against a man-made embankment. Today it has the capacity to sit thousands, and is used annually for a music and drama festival. In those early days of the Macedonian kings, a nine-day festival had been instituted here in honour of Zeus and the Muses.

Dionysos, god of wine and drama, had been popular here in northern Greece. Alexander's mother Olympias had been an ardent worshipper of the god, taking part in his ecstatic rituals. It was, no doubt, the signs and omens experienced by her just before the birth of Alexander that had encouraged him to believe himself divine, or at the very least divinely ordained.

Second to the *Iliad* Alexander had had a love of the early dramatists, and had been an admirer of Euripides many of whose plays he could recite by heart. He may well have sat in on a performance here of the *Bacchae*, a tragedy which illustrated the violent death of an unbeliever who scoffed at Dionysos' claim he was the son of Zeus. Such things would have influenced the young Alexander who, at the age of twenty-two, set out to conquer Asia.

It is appropriate that here now at Dion, as we leave the theatre and take a short-cut over the flat turf back to the path leading to the exit, we take a last look at the solid mass and craggy peaks of Olympus, the imposing backdrop to this ancient site.

Tomorrow is our final day in Litochoro, and we have no plan

except to visit the mountain one last time. The mountain with its myths and legends is a strong magnet which draws the world to it, and will do for ever, so it seems.

★

Starting again from Prionia we went over the pine-wood bridge across the gorge where we'd sat beside our rock-pool and the waterfall. It was pleasantly cool as we followed the track through the forest of deciduous trees, though the physical exertion of climbing upwards heated us to near boiling point, so we rested and drank water every hundred metres or so.

In due course we reached where the deciduous trees gave way to fir-trees and pine only. We were eventually high enough to look down on the tall firs growing vertically from the lower precipitous slopes; over them the odd puff of cloud floated. Looking higher, we glimpsed the craggy peaks against the clear blue sky, and could see fallen trees where an avalanche or rock-fall had uprooted them.

Harry called a halt and said firmly that we'd climbed high enough. It was time to celebrate that we had come as high as we had; our fitness and good health were in our favour, but our – ('age' was a forbidden word).

We sat and surveyed the scene. Achilles' mother Thetis had come to Mt. Olympus to fetch new armour for Achilles when his old armour had been filched from the body of Patroclus when Hector killed him. *...Thetis of the silver feet came to the house of Hephaestus which the god of the crooked foot had built, imperishable, starlike...a house of bronze that stands out among the dwellings of the gods. She found Hephaestus sweating as he busied himself about the bellows in his forge. He was making twenty tripods to stand round the wall of his hall...* (Iliad Bk18:367-373)

Hephaestus owed Thetis a favour as she had once taken him into her home in her cavern in the Aegean where she'd cared for him for nine years after he'd been flung from Mt. Olympus by his mother because of his deformity. Another story says he was crippled when thrown from Olympus by Zeus in a rage.

Hephaestus was eager to repay Thetis for her former kindness, and immediately *...went back to his bellows and turned them on the fire and told them to work. The bellows, there were twenty of them, blew on the crucibles sending blasts of varying force, to aid his labour according to his requirements. He cast imperishable bronze on the fire, and tin and precious* *gold and silver. Then he set a great anvil on its stand, and gripped a sturdy hammer in one hand, and in the other tongs...* (Iliad Bk18:468-477)

Within twenty-four hours he'd produced a set of well-wrought armour depicting on it the constellations and a variety of scenes from farm and city life. ...*Finally, around the uttermost rim of the cleverly-fashioned shield, he put the mighty Stream of Ocean.*

*When the shield was finished, in all its size and strength, he made Achilles a corslet brighter than a flame, and he wrought a massive helmet to fit on his temples...and put on it a crest of gold, and wrought for him greaves of pliant tin.*

*When the renowned lame god had finished all the armour, he took and laid it before the mother of Achilles. Then like a falcon she took the glittering armour from Hephaestus and swooped down with it from snow-clad Olympus.* (Iliad Bk18:607-618)

Such armour would have left any ordinary warrior staggering helplessly under its weight, but not so with Achilles who was renowned as the swiftest and most powerful warrior of all time.

I glimpsed a baseball-cap on a head moving steadily upwards along a sloping ridge far below before it disappeared from sight. High up I could see a blasted pine-tree, its stricken branches stretched out to the heavens, an image of a dying warrior.

"Have another slice of cheese," Harry offered. It was the last and he was being selfless. In his hand was half a buttered roll which I could see him eyeing hopefully.

"You have it," I said.

My mind drifted to Nicagoras, the young Greek we'd met our first morning who'd been about to climb the mountain with his girlfriend. We'd come across him at the hotel and I'd asked him if they'd achieved their goal. 'F...ing fantastic!' had been his immediate response. 'Shhhhhhh!' had been mine. How had it been in the thunderstorm, I'd asked? His brown eyes lit up at the memory. They'd been glad they'd reached the refuge-hut, unlike a couple of Americans who'd arrived drenched as they came in out of the storm. I'd wanted to know about his impressions of the summit, and he'd told us about the all round panoramic views. Yes, you could see the sea; yes, you were looking down on peaks and ridges and puffs of white cloud hanging over them. And, yes, he'd signed the f...ing visitor's book.

He'd then told us he and Liziana were planning to do the long hike to the Plateau of the Muses in a couple of days – another thing we'd never done. Homer had on several occasions appealed to them:

*...Tell me now, you Muses who have your homes on Mt. Olympus...*

I'd seen a photo of the Plateau in a book I had on hiking in the area. It was of a gently undulating treeless landscape with low clumps of vegetation. From it there was an unimpeded view to the Throne of Zeus. It was, however, a six-hour trek and said to be more difficult to do than the one to the Spilios Agapitos refuge-hut.

Harry dismissed my grumble that we hadn't reached the summit, and hadn't done the Plateau of the Muses with an airy: "So?"

I was having to learn patience and resignation.

The Plateau of the Muses, I thought wistfully – unseen! The Mytikas peak – unreached! The Throne of Zeus – ditto! So much unfinished business! So much I hadn't done – altogether unsatisfactory!

My musings were interrupted by the sound of a low-toned bell approaching. A moment later a swarthy character wearing a baseball cap and riding a mule, appeared from around a crag; several other mules laden with provisions for the refuge-hut followed behind. We exchanged greetings as they passed. The sound of the low-toned bell, of creaking saddle-packs and the pad of hooves on the track, were all that broke the silence of the mountain.

I realized suddenly that it wasn't necessary to scale the peaks to experience Mt. Olympus; at whatever height you reached you couldn't help but be a part of it.

Because Harry wanted time for another swim that afternoon, we gathered our things together and began the long trek down from the mountain of the gods, to the land of men.

I sat on the shingle beach, gazing across the Aegean, I supposed in the direction of Troy. My thoughts drifted idly to Poseidon, the great god of the sea, and I wondered what he'd make of the small mortal with one white arm, then the other, alternately appearing from the sea as he did the crawl over this, Poseidon's sacred domain, swimming back and forth, and now floating, toes up to the sky.

Poseidon had played his part in supporting the Greeks in the Trojan War. When he'd seen them in a desperate plight he'd *...harnessed to his chariot his two bronze-hooved horses, with their flowing golden manes. He clothed himself in gold, seized his well-wrought lash of gold, mounted his chariot and drove out across the waves. The sea beasts frolicked beneath him, on all sides out of the deep, for well they knew their* *lord. The sea itself stood back for him, so that his bounding horses bore him on, and the bronze axle of his chariot remained dry below as they carried him towards the Achaean fleet.* (Iliad Bk13:23-32)

It was a poetic description. He dismounted from his chariot somewhere near Tenedos then joined the Greek army where he'd instilled fresh courage and energy in the warriors so that they'd formed *...an impenetrable barrier; spear on spear, and shield on serried shield, buckler pressed on buckler, helmet to helmet, man to man. The horse-hair crests on the bright helmets touched each other as they nodded, so close they stood each by the other.*

*They looked steadily to their front and were eager for battle...* (Iliad Bk13:129-135)

I noticed the sky was yet again changing colour and the sea was a metallic green; I could see we were once more threatened with a storm. I called Harry's attention to it, and he quickly swam ashore, dried himself and dressed. We were on our hotel balcony in our ringside seats when the thunder clouds finally rolled in across the heavens towards us. This time it hailed with flash-lightning and thunder, similar to the din of battle when the gods joined in as two opposing forces *...Athena raised her war-cry, standing now by the ditch beyond the Greek wall, and now sending her voice down the thundering shore, she was answered on the other side by Ares, who raged like a black squall and screamed his orders to the Trojans... Up on high the Father of men and gods thundered ominously, and down below Poseidon caused the wide world and the lofty mountain-tops to shake...*

*Such was the cosmic crash of gods joining in conflict...* (Iliad Bk20:48-67) [P.J.& D.C.H.R.]

The storm soon passed, though clouds remained over Mt. Olympus. For a moment a break appeared in them against the soaring craggy peaks, revealing a shape looking like a flying eagle, symbol of Lord Zeus. It was there only briefly before the clouds merged again and the image vanished.

My eye moved back to the nearby church with its cross proclaiming Christianity. It had taken nearly four centuries before Zeus and his family had been eclipsed by this new religion.

But, although the pagan gods were finally defeated, they have never been forgotten; nor have the heroes of the Trojan War or the lovely Helen. Thanks to the *Iliad* and the Odyssey Homer still sings to us across the great divide of time, between his day and ours, keeping the gods, Helen and the heroes eternally alive.

# TEXT ACKNOWLEDGEMENTS

Grateful acknowledgement is made for permission to reproduce material from the following translations of Homer's *Iliad* and *Odyssey*: Peter Jones and D.C.H. Rieu revision of E.V.Rieu's translation of the *Iliad*, Penguin Classics, 2003. Richmond Lattimore's translation of the *Odyssey of Homer*, Harper Perennial Modern Classics, 1967. Walter Shewring from the *Odyssey*, Oxford University Press, 1980.

# BIBLIOGRAPHY

Baumann, Hellmut: *Greek Wild Flowers and plant lore in ancient Greece.* The Herbert Press, 1993.

Grant, Michael & John Hazel: *Who's Who in Classical Mythology.* Weidenfeld & Nicolson, 1993.

Graves, Robert: *The Greek Myths:I & II.* Penguin Books Ltd., 1986.

*Greece, the Blue Guide.* A & C Black Publishers Ltd, 1990.

*Greece, the Rough Guide.* Penguin Books, 1995.

Grigson, Geoffrey: *The Goddess of Love.* Constable & Co. Ltd., 1976.

Herodotus: *The Histories of Herodotus, translated by Harry Carter.* Oxford University Press, 1962.

Harvey, Sir Paul: *The Oxford Companion to Classical Literature.* Oxford University Press, 1974.

Hesiod: *Theogony, translated by Richard Clay.* Penguin Books Ltd., 1985.

Homer: *The Iliad, translated by Martin Hammond.* Penguin Books Ltd, 1987.

Homer: *The Iliad, tranlated by Andrew Lang.* Airmont Publishing Company Inc., 1966.

Homer: *The Iliad, translated by Richmond Lattimore.* The University of Chicago Press, 2011.

Homer: *The Iliad, translated by E.V. Rieu.* Penguin Books, 1950.

Homer: *The Iliad, originally translated by E.V. Rieu, revised and updated by Peter Jones with D.C.H. Rieu.* Penguin Books, 2003.

Homer: *The Odyssey, translated by Richmond Lattimore.* Harper Perennial, 1967.

Homer: *The Odyssey, translated by Walter Shewring.* Oxford University Press, 1980.

Homer: *The Odyssey, translated by E.V. Rieu.* Penguin Books Ltd., 1946.

Jones, Peter: *Homer's Odyssey, A commentary based on the English Translation of Richmond Lattimore*. Bristol Classical Press, 1988.

Kerényi, Carl: *Dionysos*. Princeton University Press, 1996.

Kerényi, Carl: *The Gods of the Greeks*. Penguin Books Ltd., 1958.

Kerényi, Carl: *The Heroes of the Greeks*. Thames and Hudson, 1959.

Lang, Andrew: *The Homeric Hymns (a new prose translation)*. George Allen, London, 1899.

Pausanias: *Guide to Greece, volumes 1&2*. Penguin Books Ltd., 1971.

Plato: *The Collected Dialogues of Plato*, edited by Edith Hamilton and Huntington Cairns. Princton University Press, 1961.

Radice, Betty: *Who's Who in the Ancient World*. Penguin Books, 1973.

Scully, Vincent: *The Earth, the Temple, and the Gods*. Yale University Press, 1962.

Virgil: *The Aeneid, translated by W.F. Jackson*. Penguin Books Ltd., 1956.

Willcock, Malcolm M: *A Companion to the Iliad based on the translation by Richmond Lattimore*. The University of Chicago Press, 1976.

# GLOSSARY

**ACHAEANS**
Another name used by Homer for the Greeks.

**ACHILLES**
Son of Peleus and Thetis, and Greek hero of the Trojan War.

**AEGISTHUS**
Cousin of King Agamemnon and his brother Menelaus, later to become the lover of Clytemnestra, wife of Agamemnon.

**AENEAS**
Son of Anchises, a descendant of the Royal House of Troy, and Aphrodite.

**AEOLUS**
King of the floating island of Aeolia.

**AEROPE**
Wife of King Atreus. She was seduced by his brother Thyestes.

**AESCHYLUS**
A great Athenian dramatist c.525-456 B.C.

**AGAMEMNON**
King of Mycenae and brother of Menelaus. He was commander-in-chief of the Greek army in the Trojan War.

**AJAX**
Greek hero and son of King Telamon of Salamis.

**ALCINOUS**

King of the mythical Phaeacians (thought to be Corfu), and father of Nausicaa.

**ALEXANDER THE GREAT (356-323 B.C.)**

King of Macedonia, son of Philip II and Olympias.

**AMPHITRITE**

Wife of Poseidon.

**ANCHISES**

A Trojan prince/shepherd on Mt. Ida loved by Aphrodite. Their son was Aeneas.

**ANDROMACHE**

Wife of King Priam of Troy's son Hector.

**ANTICLEA**

Mother of Odysseus, and wife of King Laertes.

**APHRODITE**

Goddess of love. In the Trojan War she supported the Trojans.

**APOLLO**

Son of Zeus and Leto, and twin brother of Artemis. He was god of music, archery and prophecy. In the Trojan War he supported the Trojans.

**ARES**

God of war. He supported the Trojans.

**ARGONAUTS**

The heroes who joined Jason in the ship the *Argo* on his quest for the Golden Fleece.

**ARGUS**

A monster with a hundred eyes.

**ARTEMIS**

Daughter of Zeus and Leto, and twin sister of Apollo. She was goddess of wild life and hunting, as well as defender of young children. She supported the Trojans in the Trojan War.

**ASCLEPIUS**

God of medicine and healing, son of Apollo. His two sons Machaon and Podalirius joined the Greek army and tended the wounded in the Trojan War.

**ATHENA**

Daughter of Zeus. She was born mature and fully armed from his head. She was goddess of handicraft, and protectress of many cities, but especially of Athens. She was the embodiment of wisdom. In the Trojan War she supported the Greeks.

**BALIUS**

One of two immortal horses given by the gods to Peleus on his marriage, afterwards by Peleus to Achilles when he set out for the Trojan War.

**BOREAS**

The north wind.

**BRISEIS**

A Trojan slave-girl won in battle by Achilles.

**CALCHAS**

A seer and priest of Apollo who accompanied King Agamemnon to the war.

**CALYPSO**

An enchantress who bewitched Odysseus on his homeward journey; he stayed with her seven years till Zeus intervened and sent him on his way.

**CASSANDRA**

Daughter of King Priam and Hecuba. She had the gift of prophecy though no one ever believed her.

**CASTOR**

See Dioscuri.

**CENTAURS**

Mythical beasts, half-man, half-horse who lived on Mt. Pelion.

**CHARICLO**

Wife of the centaur Cheiron.

**CHARON**

The ferryman who was believed to row the dead across the river Styx to Hades.

**CHARYBDIS**

A perilous whirlpool opposite Scylla near Sicily.

**CHEIRON**

A centaur who was both wise and kind and knowledgeable in music, archery and medicine.

**CHRYSES**

Priest of Apollo, and father of Chryseis, Agamemnon's slave-girl.

**CHRYSEIS**

Daughter of Chryses, priest of Apollo, who became King Agamemnon's slave-girl.

**CIRCE**

An enchantress with whom Odysseus spent a year on his journey home from Troy.

**CLYTEMNESTRA**

Wife of King Agamemnon, and sister of Helen. She took Aegisthus for her lover, and murdered her husband on his return from the Trojan War.

**CREUSA**

Wife of Aeneas. She died when the Greeks set fire to Troy.

**CYCLOPES**

One-eyed giants who made thunderbolts for Zeus.

**DARDANIANS**

Another name used by Homer for the Trojans.

**DEIPHOBUS**

Son of King Priam and Hecuba. He married Helen after the death of Paris.

**DIOMEDES**

Greek hero of the Trojan War, and son of King Tydeus of Argos.

**DIONYSOS**

Son of Zeus and the mortal woman Semele. He was god of wine and drama.

**DIOSCURI**

Castor and Polydeuces, the 'heavenly twins'. They were the sons of Zeus and Leda, and brothers of Helen and Clytemnestra.

**ELECTRA**

Daughter of King Menelaus and Clytemnestra.

**ERIS**
The personification of Strife or Discord.

**EUMAEUS**
Swineherd to Odysseus.

**EURYCLEIA**
Odysseus' old nurse.

**GAEA**
Personification of the earth.

**HADES**
Brother of Zeus and god of the underworld.

**HECTOR**
Son of King Priam and his wife Hecuba, and brother of Paris.

**HECUBA**
Wife of King Priam of Troy, and mother of Hector, Helenus, Deiphobus and Paris.

**HELEN**
Daughter of Leda and Zeus. She became the wife of Menelaus, and they had a daughter Hermione. She was seduced by Paris and ran away with him to Troy which triggered the Trojan War.

**HELENUS**
A seer son of King Priam and Hecuba. When Paris was killed, he wanted to marry Helen and, because his brother Deiphobus married her, turned traitor.

**HEPHAESTUS**
Lame son of Zeus and Hera. He was god of fire and a master craftsman in metal-work. When requested he supported the Greeks in the war.

**HERA**
Wife of Zeus, goddess of women and marriage. She supported the Greeks in the Trojan War.

**HERMES**
Son of Zeus and the mortal woman Maia. He was his father's messenger in the war, and conducted the souls of the dead to Hades.

**HERMIONE**
Daughter of Menelaus and Helen. She was nine years old when her mother ran off with Paris.

**HOMER**

A blind bard and composer of the two epic poems the *Iliad* and the *Odyssey*. He was believed to have lived c.700 B.C.

**HYAKINTHUS**

A handsome youth of Amyklae near Sparta, beloved of Apollo as well as Zephyrus (the west wind).

**ILIUM**

Another name by which Troy was known.

**IO**

Hera's priestess at Argos.

**IPHIGENIA**

Daughter of King Agamemnon and Clytemnestra. Her father sacrificed her at Aulis in Greece in order to appease Artemis who was preventing the Greek ships from setting sail for Troy.

**IRIS**

Goddess of the rainbow and messenger of the gods.

**IXION**

King of the Lapiths. He fell in love with Hera, whereupon Zeus fashioned a cloud in his wife's image which Ixion promptly seduced. For this crime Zeus condemned him to Tartarus bound to a wheel which rotated for ever.

**JASON**

Son of the king of Iolchos. His uncle usurped the throne and, knowing through an oracle that he was destined to be killed by Jason, he promised to give up the throne if he brought him back the Golden Fleece from Colchis.

**KAZ DAGI**

The Turkish name for Gargarus on Mt. Ida.

**KRONOS**

Son of Ouranos (sky) and Gaia (earth), Rhea was his wife and they gave birth to the major Olympian Gods.

**LAERTES**

King of Ithaka and father of Odysseus.

**LAOCOON**

A Trojan priest of Apollo (some say of Poseidon).

**LAPITHS**

A race from north Thessaly, they are often depicted on temple friezes doing battle with the centaurs.

**LEDA**

Wife of King Tyndareus of Sparta, and mother of Clytemnestra and the Dioscuri.

**MENELAUS**

Son of King Atreus of Mycenae, and brother of Agamemnon. He became king of Sparta when he married Helen.

**MUSES**

Nine daughters of Zeus and Mnemosyne (personification of Memory). Each presided over one of the arts or sciences.

**NAUPLIOS**

A son of Poseidon. He was an early navigator and founded the port of Nauflio in the Peloponnese.

**NEOPTOLEMUS**

Son of Achilles, sometimes known as Pyrrhus.

**NEREIDS**

Daughters of Nereus. Sea-deities, one of whom was Thetis who became the mother of Achilles.

**NESTOR**

King of Pylos, and the eldest of the Greek warriors; he was considered the wisest and his advice was always listened to.

**ODYSSEUS**

Son of King Laertes of Ithaka. He was married to Penelope and they had one son, Telemachus. Odysseus was one of the most courageous and daring of the Greek warriors; it was he who master-minded the stealing of the Trojan *palladium* and the construction of the Wooden Horse. Homer's *Odyssey* tells of his perilous journey home from Troy which took ten years.

**OENONE**

A nymph on Mt. Ida to whom Paris was first married.

**ORESTES**

Son of King Agamemnon and Clytemnestra. After the murder of his father by his mother, Orestes killed his mother to avenge his father's murder.

**PALAMEDES**

One of the Greek heroes from the small port of Nauflio in the Peloponnese. He was the son of Nauplios.

**PALLADIUM**

The Trojan *palladium* was said to have descended from heaven. It was a wooden image of the goddess Athena and was kept in her temple in the city of Troy. So long as it remained there the safety of Troy was assured. It was why Odysseus set out to steal it.

**PARIS**

Son of the King of Troy. It was his selection of Aphrodite at the Judgement, and her promise to give him the most beautiful woman in the world, that triggered the Trojan War.

**PATROCLUS**

Childhood friend of Achilles.

**PEISISTRATUS**

Son of King Nestor.

**PELEUS**

King of Phthia, married to Thetis, a Nereid and sea-goddess. Achilles was their son.

**PHAEACIA**

An island, believed to be Corfu.

**PHOENIX**

Sent by King Peleus to be guardian and adviser to the young Achilles at the outset of the Trojan War.

**POLYPHEMUS**

A one-eyed Cyclops who imprisoned Odysseus and his men in the *Odyssey*. Odysseus managed to blind him, and so escaped.

**POSEIDON**

Brother of Zeus. He was god of the sea as well as of earthquakes and horses. He supported the Greeks in the war.

**PRIAM**

King of Troy married to Hecuba. They had ten sons, the most famous being Paris and Hector.

**PROTEUS**

The 'Old Man of the Sea' who was able to assume different shapes.

**PYRRHUS**

See Neoptolemus

**SCAMANDER**

A major river of the Trojan plain.

**SCHLIEMANN, Heinrich (1822-1890 A.D.)**

A self-made German millionnaire. He was an enthusiastic amateur archaeologist, obsessed with the major sites mentioned in the *Iliad* and the *Odyssey*.

**SCYLLA**

A monster in the Straits of Messina opposite Charybdis. Odysseus had to sail past these two dangers. Scylla was said to have six heads, each head with a mouth containing triple rows of teeth, and a ring of barking dogs around her stomach.

**SINON**

Greek hero who infiltrated the Trojan lines and by misinformation helped to bring about the downfall of Troy.

**SIRENS**

Weird women who lured sailors to their doom by their singing.

**STYX**

The river across which the dead were ferried to Hades.

**TANTALUS**

Father of Pelops. For his murder of Pelops and for serving him up in a dish to the gods, he was condemned to hunger and thirst for eternity.

**TARTARUS**

The underworld where the souls of sinners went after judgement.

**TELEMACHUS**

Son of Odysseus.

**THETIS**

A goddess and sea-nymph, daughter of Nereus. She married King Peleus of Phthia and Achilles was their son. It was at their wedding that Eris threw down a golden apple with the words on it 'for the fairest' which triggered the Trojan War.

**THYESTES**

Son of Pelops and Hippodamia, and brother of Atreus who became King of Mycenae.

**TROAD**

The historical name for the area in north-west Turkey around Troy.

**TUMULUS**

A burial mound.

**TYNDAREUS**

King of Sparta married to Leda.

**WOODEN HORSE**

A wooden structure in which the best Greek warriors concealed themselves to gain entry to the city of Troy which brought about its final destruction.

**XANTHUS**

One of Achilles' two immortal horses given by the gods to his father King Peleus on his marriage.

**ZEPHYRUS**

The west wind.

**ZEUS**

Supreme god of the ancient world. In the Trojan War he sometimes supported the Trojans, sometimes the Greeks.

# INDEX

ALSO BY JILL DUDLEY:

Ye Gods!
*(Travels in Greece)*

Ye Gods! II
*(More travels in Greece)*

Holy Smoke!
*(Travels in Turkey and Egypt)*

Gods in Britain
*(An island odyssey from pagan to Christian)*

Mortals and Immortals
*(A satirical fantasy & true-in-parts memoir)*

Holy Fire!
*(Travels in the Holy Land)*

Lap of the Gods
*(Travels in Crete and the Aegean Islands)*

# BIOGRAPHY

Jill Dudley was born in Baghdad and educated in England. Her first play was performed by the Leatherhead Repertory Company, since when she has written plays and short stories for radio. She returned to Iraq in 1956 when her husband was working out there and after the Iraqi revolution they came back to England where they bought a dairy farm. When they retired from farming in 1990 they travelled extensively around Greece, Turkey and Egypt and a number of her travel articles have appeared in the national newspapers followed in quick succession by her popular travel-writing books.